ADVANCED EVERYDAY ENGLISH

by Steven Collins

ADVANCED STUDENTS OF ENGLISH

You will never find a better series of books to help you improve your vocabulary

ISBN 978-0-9528358-9-9

www.learnenglishadvanced.com

Montserrat Publishing

MONTSERRAT PUBLISHING
Advanced Everyday English

Copyright © 2011 Steven Collins

First edition 2011
Second edition 2012
Third edition 2014
Fourth edition 2020

Montserrat Publishing
practicalenglish@hotmail.co.uk

Illustrations
Alex Stead
www.alexsteadart.com
info@alexsteadart.com

Typesetting & Cover Design
Deaths by Coconut Studio

Editing and proofreading
Gavin Best
bestgav@hotmail.com

www.learnenglishadvanced.com

To my boy-chik, Daniel (D.C.R)

Steven Collins was born in London in 1960. He grew up in Harrow and qualified as a lawyer (solicitor) in 1987, having done a Master's in Law at Trinity Hall, Cambridge. He then decided to make a complete change of career and went into T.E.F.L. (Teaching English as a Foreign Language). Having lived and taught in Italy and Spain, he returned to London in 1993 to write this book and to open his own school in Central London, specialising in practical English for advanced students. However, in 2008 he retired from teaching to concentrate full time on writing and publishing.

Introduction
ADVANCED EVERYDAY ENGLISH
Steven Collins

Thank you for buying Advanced Everyday English, the second book in the Practical Everyday English series.

It is designed in very much the same mode as the first one (Practical Everyday English) in that all of the examples will contain vocabulary and expressions you have studied on earlier pages. You will also find many words from the first book, which will give you an opportunity to revise the material. In this second book there is more of what one might call "serious" vocabulary, but there are plenty of phrasal verbs and idioms as well.

The book will be of particular benefit to those readers with an advanced level of English who wish to become (or who already are) interpreters, translators or teachers of English, or who simply want to be able to speak and understand English at a very high level. In addition, people who need to read English language journals or converse in English on a daily basis, either in business or for pleasure, will find it very useful.

Once again I have included dialogue and exercises at the end of each chapter, so that you can see how the words are used in free conversation and writing, and test yourself on what you have studied in each chapter. Like the first book, there are three lessons in each chapter and nine chapters in total. My suggestion is to read one lesson a week and then do a revision after finishing each chapter. I hope you enjoy the illustrations too.

It is my sincere wish that, together with the first book, you find Advanced Everyday English an invaluable tool in perfecting your English language skills.

Good luck!

Steven Collins

For more information about the Practical Everyday English series, visit:
www.learnenglishadvanced.com

Lesson One

Outgoing

i. (Sociable, open and friendly, not shy--*not to be confused with "**outgoings**", which means personal or business expenses such as rent and domestic bills*)
Examples:

- Job Advertisement:
  Outgoing *Sales Assistant required. Must be on the ball and capable of taking on hectic work schedule.*
- *In the long run, you'll pick up more clients if you adopt a more* **outgoing** *attitude.*
- *The place needed doing up, but it wasn't that which put us off going for it: the* **outgoings** *were outrageous.*

ii. (Used to describe someone who is about to retire from a high position, e.g. president, chairman)
Example:

- *Virtually the whole town turned out to see off the* **outgoing** *president; they weren't particularly looking forward to meeting the new one.*

iii. (A collection of mail which is to be sent, rather than "incoming", which has just been received)
Example:

- *I'm sorry to be bossy, but letters which are to go off should be put in the '***outgoing***' tray.*

Off the record (Unofficially, "Don't tell anybody I said this, but…", not to be made public--*note the opposite "**on record**", which means official, a publicly known fact*)

Examples:

- Mortgage Consultant:
  You could wind up paying higher interest.
  Off the record, *I reckon you'd be better off going to your own bank rather than one of my clients.*
- *Before we get things under way, I must stress that anything that comes up during this meeting must be kept strictly* **off the record.**
- Interviewer to Prime Minister:
  I'm not trying to catch you out, but you are **on record** *as saying that inflation would plummet once we had recovered from the slump.*

To go by

i. (To rely on/ judge something by what one has heard, seen or read
--*often used in the negative--note also* **"to go by the book"**, *which
means to stick to the rules*)
Examples:

- You can't **go by** what he comes out with; you need to seek
  a specialist who caters for experienced professionals.
- I never **go by** the tabloid press; mind you, this latest scandal
  is quite an eye-opener. The outgoing mayor had clearly been
  up to something.
- We do try to **go by the book** in this company, but, off
  the record, the odd rule gets broken from time to time.

ii. (To pass--*used for time only*)
Examples:

- As time **goes by,** I feel we're drifting apart.
- Five years **went by** without me hearing from him, and
  then out of the blue, he turned up at the house.

To baffle (To confuse, puzzle)

Examples:

- Computers really **baffle** me; I'm not cut out for the modern
  age at all.
- I was **baffled** by her behaviour. What do you think came
  over her?

Hardship (A state or period of suffering caused by a lack of money, a sacrifice--
generally experienced when having to give up something pleasant)

Examples:

- We had to put up with far worse **hardships** when we
  were children, so don't make out you're hard-done by.
- I could do without biscuits quite happily, but cutting out
  chocolate would definitely be a **hardship**.

To be in one's element (To feel comfortable in a certain situation, to enjoy doing something because it is exactly right and suitable for that person)

Examples:
- As an outgoing person, I'm **in my element** when I have to make a speech off the top of my head in front of a crowd of people.
- She dropped out of her business course and has now taken up a fine arts degree. She's really **in her element** now.

*"Computers really **baffle** me; I'm not cut out for the modern age at all."*
(see page 2)

To brush up (To improve one's knowledge on a particular subject, to revise)

Examples:
- I thought I could get by in Spanish, but as it turned out, I needed to do quite a bit of **brushing up**.
- You'd better **brush up** on your general knowledge before putting yourself down for the college quiz.

Touchy (Over-sensitive, easily upset or annoyed. A subject which is likely to upset someone)

Examples:

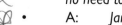
- Just because I had a go at you last night, there's no need to be so **touchy.**
- A: Jane's very **touchy**, but her sister is quite thick-skinned.
- B: Oh, I wouldn't go along with that at all. It's the other way around!
- It's a very **touchy** subject; I wouldn't bring it up if I were you.

3

Cliché (An expression, viewpoint or idea which has been used so many times that it has become boring and has lost its effect--*this is a French word which, like many others, has come into everyday English usage*)

Examples:
- *It's unheard of for the manager of a football team not to come out with the same old* **clichés**.
- *I know it's a* **cliché**, *but what you get out of this life depends on what you put into it.*

To lay out

i. (To present something in a clear way, to arrange things so that they can be easily seen)
Examples:

- *It's imperative that we* **lay out** *our main proposals in the booklet, otherwise the message might not come across.*
- *If you* **lay** *everything* **out** *on the table, it will be easier to sort out what papers are worth keeping.*

ii. (To design, plan a building, town, etc--*note the noun "**layout**", which is the way in which something is designed or arranged*)
Examples:
- *The garden is clearly* **laid out** *in my mind. The only drawback is that I know I'll never get round to doing anything about it.*
- *In her latest job they've asked her to take on the responsibility of* **laying out** *the new town centre. She will be in her element.*
- *The lack of light can be put down to the poor* **layout** *of the building.*
- *I'm not keen on the* **layout** *of the follow-up brochure; it's bound to baffle many of our customers.*

iii. (To pay for something/spend a lot of money reluctantly--*see "**to fork/shell out**", Practical Everyday English page 168*) **Colloquial**
Examples:
- Wife to husband:
  If your car has got so much going for it, why have we had to **lay out** *£1,000 before it's even got through its first six months?*
- *Your brother is always making out that he's had a life of hardship, but quite frankly, I'm fed up with having to* **lay out** *for him.*

Lesson Two

To go about

i. (To approach/deal with a problem or situation in a particular way--*often used with "how"*)
Examples:

- *Even though I've been running my own business for quite a long while now, I still haven't got a clue as to <u>how</u> to **go about** giving someone the sack.*
- *It seems to be a sensible way of **going about** it; mind you, it baffles me as to why it has taken this long to get things under way.*

ii. (To circulate--*often used with "rumour" or a non-life-threatening virus*)
Examples:

- *There's a rumour **going about** – strictly off the record of course – that more redundancies are in the pipeline.*
- A: *I think I'm coming down with something.*
  B: *You've probably picked up the flu bug that's **going about** at the moment.*

Loophole (A gap or mistake in a particular law/rule which allows people to avoid having to obey it)

Examples:

- *Our solicitor is bound to find a **loophole** enabling us to get round the law.*
- *Interviewer to politician:*
  *You're on record as saying that people have got away with murder for far too long and that the obvious **loopholes** in the law must be tightened up.*

 # To keep someone posted (To keep someone up-to-date with the news/ what is going on)

Examples:

- *All the amendments are clearly laid out in this document, but we'll **keep you posted** on anything else which crops up.*
- *If you had **kept me posted** instead of dithering around, we wouldn't have had all this mess to sort out.*

To break even (Not to make a profit or a loss)

Examples:
- We reckoned that we'd just about **break even** in the first year, but, as it turned out, business really took off.
- I know it's a cliché, but during a slump you should count yourself lucky if you can **break even**.

Backlog (A large amount of work which has been building up over a period of time, a lot of people waiting to be dealt with or seen)

Examples:
- I've got a **backlog** of paperwork to get through before I can turn my mind to these other issues.
- There's a **backlog** of people to see, but, off the record, if you turn up before nine, we should be able to fit you in.

To rub someone up the wrong way (To irritate/annoy someone)

Examples:
- Perhaps I'm being too touchy, but there's something about that man that **rubs me up the wrong way.**
- He really knows how to **rub her up the wrong way.** Why does she stand for it?

To come through

i. (To pull through/survive a difficult period of time, to progress through a training period)

Examples:
- We had to put up with a lot of hardships during our time in the army but we all **came through** it in the end.
- Football coach:
  Our star players have not been up to scratch this season; mind you, we've got quite a number of youngsters **coming through.**

ii. (To be evident/apparent)

Examples:
- What **came through** most of all was his reluctance to come to terms with the truth.
- His nasty streak only **comes through** when he's being rubbed up the wrong way.

iii. (to arrive after having been processed--*usually documents*)
Examples:
- We can't put out these brochures until the new lease **comes through**.
- The Home Office have told me that because of a backlog of applications, my visa is unlikely to **come through** until the new year.

*"Our star players have not been up to scratch this season; mind you, we've got quite a number of youngsters **coming through**."*
(see page 6)

To give someone (a lot of) stick, to get/take (a lot of) stick (To tease, make fun of, criticise continually, to be teased, criticised continually--*note also "to come in for stick", which can be used in the same way as "to take stick"*) **Colloquial**

Examples:
- We **give him a lot of stick** at work over his appalling choice of ties, but he is too thick-skinned to let it bother him.
- I got **relentless stick** last time I went in for the marathon, so I am not putting my name down for it this year.
- Film critic appearing on television:
  I've t**aken quite a bit of stick** this week from viewers for slagging off Dustin Hoffman's latest film, so I'm going to steer clear of the matter on tonight's programme.
- The Board of Directors **came in for a lot of stick** over the way they handled such a touchy issue.

To be up in the air (To be uncertain/unsettled)

Examples:
- A: *How's your new office coming along?*

  B: *Everything's **up in the air** at the moment;*
     I haven't got a clue what's going on.
- *We've sorted out the costings, but the layout is all **up in the air**.*

Dogsbody (A person who is employed to do menial jobs only)

Examples:
- *I'm sorry, but I won't let you get away with treating me like your **dogsbody** any more.*
- *Initially, he was taken on just as a general **dogsbody**, which is why no-one can get over his promotion to Regional Manager.*

Lesson Three

To go round

i. (To go to someone's home--see *"**to go over**", Practical Everyday English, page 12, meaning i*)
Example:
- I'm **going round** to John's to give him some stick about his team losing the Cup Final. That will really rub him up the wrong way.

ii. (To socialise/go out with a person or people on a regular basis--*generally used by children and young adults*) **Colloquial**
Examples:
- I don't really **go around/round** with my college friends these days; we've drifted apart in recent years.
- One child to another:
  I know we get on well with each other, but my mum has told me that I'm not allowed to **go around** with you any more.

iii. (To spread, to get round--*see Practical Everyday English, page 167, meaning ii*
--, *to go about*-- *see earlier, page 5, meaning ii*)
Examples:
- The stories that **went round** about these two guys were a real eye-opener.
- There's a stomach bug **going round** the school at the moment, so many of our kids are feeling a bit under the weather.

iv. (To be in the habit of doing something or to behave in a certain way which is generally disapproved of)
Examples:
- If you **go round** deliberately winding everyone up, people are bound to get hold of the wrong end of the stick.
- I don't **go round** treating my employees like dogsbodies, and I don't expect you to try it on either.

v. To have a sufficient quantity of something for everyone to enjoy/use--*often used with "enough" or "plenty"*)
Examples:
- In the past we took it for granted that there was always <u>enough</u> money **to go round**, but these days it's a wonder that we can afford to do anything at all.
- I thought we had run out of brochures, but, as it turned out, there are <u>plenty</u> **to go round.**

One child to another: *"I know we get on well with each other, but my mum has told me that I'm not allowed to **go around/round** with you any more."*

(see page 9)

To have it in one (To possess a certain characteristic which one was not previously aware of--*often used with "I didn't know". Note also the colloquial expression "**to have it in for someone**", which means to be determined that someone will suffer, have a hard time or fail in some way, often for no apparent reason. It is not generally used in the first person; i.e. one would not say "I've got it in for him", although one might hear, "He thinks I've got it in for him"*)

Examples:
- *She's not normally so outgoing; I never believed she
had it in her to perform in front of such a big audience.*
- *John can vouch for my usual calm, easy-going nature.
<u>I didn't know</u> I **had it in me** to fly off the handle like that.*
- *I might as well give in my notice; the boss **has had it in for me**
ever since I told him he was highly strung.*

- *Every application I've made has been turned down.
  Someone **has** clearly **got it in for me**!*

Cocky (Too confident or sure that one knows everything) **Colloquial**

Examples:
- *One day I'm going to show her up in front of her friends.
  I won't stand for her **cocky** attitude any longer.*
- *It served him right when she cut him down to size. He's far
  too **cocky** for his own good.*
- *He comes over as too **cocky**. I don't think he'll fit in with
  the other members of staff.*

To bog down/to get bogged down (To prevent progress, to confuse people by giving them too much work or information, to get stuck/to be slowed down, often because of too much work)

Examples:
- *We've got to get our marketing spot-on and not bog potential
  customers **down** with too much information.*

- *I'm sorry I didn't get back to you yesterday but I got **bogged
  down** with a backlog of paperwork I had to catch up on.*

Understatement (A statement which does not go far enough or is not as strong as it should be -- *the opposite of exaggeration*)

Examples:

- *To say that my French is not up to scratch is an **understatement**.*
- A: *Our team didn't put up much of a fight today.*
  B: *That must be the **understatement** of the year.
      They were absolutely dreadful!*

Up and coming (Someone/something who/which is new and likely to be successful/popular in the near future)

Examples:
- *I feel most of the old directors are no longer on the ball; mind
  you, we've got one or two **up and coming** youngsters on the
  board who could pull us through this bad patch.*
- A: *What's **up and coming** in the fashion world at the moment?*
  B: *I haven't got a clue; I drifted away from that
      scene ages ago.*

To get going

i. (To get a move on--*see Practical Everyday English, page 183*, to hurry up and leave/start, to get something started--*note that "**to get a move on**" is preferred to "**to get going**" for use in the imperative-see 3rd example below.*)
Colloquial
Examples:

- *I'm not trying to drop you a hint, but you'd better **get going** if you want to dodge the rush hour traffic.*
- *Let's **get** this meeting **going** before we wind up having to stay the night here.*
- ***Get a move on!** We'll never clear this backlog at this rate.*

ii. (To become or make something more lively, e.g. a party) **Colloquial**
Examples:

- A: *I might have known you'd turn up late!*
- B: *Oh sorry, but we thought the party wouldn't really **get going** until midnight.*
- *We could have done with a live band **to get** the wedding reception **going** but we had to make do with background classical music instead.*

iii. (To wind up--*see Practical Everyday English, page 147, meaning iv*, to tease)
Colloquial
Example:

- *It's so easy **to get your brother going**; I never knew he was so touchy.*

To pencil someone/something in (To make a provisional [something which could be changed later] appointment with someone)

Examples:

- *I tell you what; I'll **pencil you in** for Tuesday the 18th, and in the meantime I'd appreciate it if you could keep me posted as to what's likely to come up before then.*

- *Things are a little up in the air at the moment. If you **pencil the meeting in** for Wednesday, I'll get back to you before packing up tonight on whether I can make it or not.*

At stake (At risk -- often money or one's reputation)

Examples:

- Lawyer to Client:
  *I'm sorry to be blunt, but it's not worth putting my career at **stake** over such a borderline case.*

- *Has it dawned on you exactly how much money is at **stak**e here?*

Scapegoat (A person who is unfairly blamed for everything that has gone wrong in order to satisfy public anger--*often used with the verb "to make"*)

Examples:
- *It's unfair to <u>make</u> the Chancellor the **scapegoat** for the downturn in the economy; the entire Government has got a lot to answer for.*
- *The police came off very badly in this case, having dithered for what seems an eternity, and now they are looking for a **scapegoat**.*

INTERVIEW WITH FOOTBALL MANAGER TED DAVIES

INTERVIEWER: *Good afternoon, Ted. Welcome to the show.*

DAVIES: *Thanks very much, I'm delighted to be here.*

INTERVIEWER: *Let me start by asking you a few background questions. Is it true that you were first taken on by Winchester United as a dogsbody?*

DAVIES: *Well, that's quite right. As a youngster, I used to go round with the chairman's son, and one day his father offered me the job of cleaning the players' boots. All the guys today give me a lot of stick about it. But I was a cocky lad even then. I knew I had it in me to climb the ladder. I always felt in my element at this club.*

INTERVIEWER: *Many people are baffled as to why you never made it as a regular first team player. You are on record as saying that you were occasionally played out of position.*

DAVIES: *That must be the understatement of the year. I only ever featured as a defender, which really rubbed me up the wrong way, since I was a gifted winger.*
The problem was, I didn't know how to go about adapting to new positions.

INTERVIEWER: *In today's team you seem to have a lot of young players coming through. How do you encourage them?*

DAVIES: *I try not to bog them down with technicalities. Some of them are quite touchy when I have a go at them for something. Others need a lot of pushing to get them going. I know it's a cliché, but they will all have to go through a lot of hardship before they get to the top.*

INTERVIEWER: *Thanks for your time. Good luck for the championship.*

NEWSREADER: *Good evening. This is the six o'clock news. Today the outgoing Home Secretary denied reports that the backlog of passport applications has caused millions of holidaymakers to miss their flights. He said, "You cannot go by the scare stories of the press. Everything is under control." However, a spokesman for the Travellers' Bureau said, "There's a rumour going about that the Prime Minister has admitted, off the record, that all decisions as to how to solve the problem have been left up in the air." We will, of course, keep all listeners posted.*

In other news, Members of Parliament (MPs) have been told to brush up on their European languages. There has been a survey conducted in the House of Commons questioning new members on their foreign language abilities. What came through most of all was that only a few of the up and coming politicians could get by in a foreign tongue. Some of these were even proficient enough to find loopholes in European legislation written in French. However, the majority of MPs only spoke English, and struggled with basic grammar and punctuation even in their own language. They were urged to pencil in dates for language tuition courses. The Minister for European Affairs warned the House that there was a lot at stake in Europe, and that we couldn't afford to be able to converse in only one language.

Chapter One: **Exercise**

CHOOSE THE CORRECT WORD FROM THOSE IN RED
Answers on page 133

1. *I don't think he had anything to do with what happened. They used him as ᵃ(scapegoat/ dogsbody/loophole/cliché) just because he's the office ᵇ(scapegoat/dogsbody/backlog/cocky).*

2. *You can't ᵃ(come through/go by/go around/bog down) what he says; he has never experienced any form of ᵇ(cliché/loophole/backlog/hardship) in his entire life.*

3. *You are ᵃ(on record/off the record/bogged down/at stake) as saying that he is the best of the ᵇ(understated/cocky/outgoing/up and coming) footballers, even though he's had an appalling season so far. Be prepared to ᶜ(lay out/break even/ get a lot of stick/get going) from the viewers of this show.*

4. *I didn't think you ᵃ(laid out/were in your element/had it in you/were so baffled) to be so nasty. You really ᵇ(got going/rubbed him up the wrong way/kept him posted/pencilled him in).*

5. *Last year was a hard time in our business when we weren't ᵃ(breaking even/in our element/ going around/brushing up), but look how things have picked up so dramatically this year. I don't know how we ᵇ(went about/got going/ went around/came through) such a difficult patch.*

6. *I will ᵃ(come through/go by/pencil you in/get going) for Thursday, but I do have a ᵇ(cliché/ backlog/loophole/dogsbody) of paperwork to catch up on. I've allowed myself to get a bit ᶜ(bogged down/up in the air/touchy/loopholed) with it all.*

7. *ᵃ(On record/Off the record/At stake/Coming through), the Prime Minister has admitted that there is not much he can do about the ᵇ(backlogs/scapegoats/understatements/loopholes) in the law which allow criminals to get away with murder…sometimes literally, but he keeps telling journalists that he is ᶜ(baffled/bogged down/on record/outgoing) as to why the previous government did nothing about it.*

8. *You say he is ᵃ(dogsbody/scapegoat/outgoing/up in the air). That's a bit of an ᵇ(off the record/loophole/cliché/understatement). He's a big ᶜ(cocky/touchy/bogged down/laid out) show-off!*

9. *He'll be ᵃ(kept posted/baffled/in his element/touchy) at the party with all those pretentious academics coming out with all the usual ᵇ(layouts/dogsbodies/clichés/backlogs). But don't tell him I said that; you know how ᶜ(cocky/touchy/baffled/bogged down) he can be.*

10. *There's a rumour ᵃ(going round/coming through/breaking even/up and coming) the office that you're not very keen on the new ᵇ(understatement/layout/backlog/cliché) of the building I have proposed.*

11.   *It's all a bit* ^a*(at stake/outgoing/off the record/up in the air) at the moment. I'll* ^b*(rub you up the wrong way/give you stick/keep you posted/get you bogged down) and let you know how things proceed.*

12.   *There's an awful lot* ^a*(at stake/in our element/up and coming/of dogsbodies) here. It's clear that we're all going to need to* ^b*(give a lot of stick/brush up/go round/come through) on our negotiating skills if we're going to succeed.*

13.   *I don't really know how to* ^a*(go around/go about/come through/get going) telling him our relationship is over…but I'd better* ^b*(pencil him in/rub him up the wrong way/get going/ go about) if I'm going to catch him before his train leaves.*

Lesson One

To miss out (To omit or leave out, to forget to include)

Examples:
- *I got so bogged down with the first few chapters of her book that I decided to **miss out** the middle and went straight to the end, but then I couldn't be bothered with that either.*
- *When I was going through the list of people who've been invited, I noticed I had **missed out** your uncle Tom. Whatever came over me?*

To miss out on (To miss the opportunity of doing something enjoyable or beneficial--*Note the expression "**to miss the boat**", which has a very similar meaning except that the opportunity has usually been lost because one has not acted quickly enough. It is often used to describe someone who is now considered to have left it too late to find a partner in life.*)

Examples:
- Advertisement for a legal book at a discounted price: *Don't **miss out** on this one-off opportunity to get to grips with English Company Law.*
- *If you don't turn up, you are bound to **miss out** on all the fun.*
- *My sister reckons she's **missed the boat** just because she's over 35, but in reality she's got so much going for her…and these days it's never too late to meet someone special.*

Gist (The main point of what someone is saying, the general sense of a conversation/speech, etc.)

Examples:
- *There were some words which I couldn't make out, but I got the **gist** of what he was going on about.*
- *The **gist** of his speech was that he felt hard-done-by for having been made the scapegoat...but I hope he doesn't turn to me for help.*

To ask after (To ask how someone is through a third person)

Examples:
- *Jane keeps **asking after** your brother. I'm sure she fancies him.*

- The boss was **asking after** you this morning, but don't let it go to your head.

Over-the-top (Too much, excessive)

Examples:
- Having a go at him would have sufficed; suing him was going a bit **over-the-top**.
- '**Over-the-top**' is an understatement: we could have done without three quarters of the food we ordered.

Deep down (Under/Beneath the surface, i.e. the true character or feelings that someone has rather than what he first appears to have)

Examples:
- He might make out that he takes it all in his stride, but **deep down** he can't cope with what's going on.
- Even though she comes over as a ruthless boss, **deep down** she's quite easy-going.

Once in a blue moon (Very occasionally--note that this expression is generally used in a manner of complaint about the rarity of the event)

Examples:
- **Once in a blue moon** he scores a spectacular goal, but when it comes down to it, he's not what he's cracked up to be
- Husband to wife:
  H: I don't know why you're making such a fuss; I always give you money to splash out on clothes
  W: **Once in a blue moon!**

To have a lot/enough on one's plate (To have a lot of work to get through/problems to sort out)

Examples:
- Lawyer to client:
  I'd be delighted to take your case on but **I've got such a lot on my plate** at the moment, I'd never be able to fit it in.
- 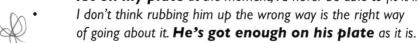 I don't think rubbing him up the wrong way is the right way of going about it. **He's got enough on his plate** as it is.

To draw out

i.   (To withdraw money from one's bank)
Example:
- *Have you already got through that money you **drew out** yesterday?*

ii.   (To lengthen a speech, lecture, etc--*generally unnecessarily. Note also the adjective "**drawn-out**" which describes something which lasts too long*)
Examples:

- *If you run short of ideas, you can always **draw out** the seminar with some witty stories…but don't bog the audience down with financial statistics.*
- *I could have done without him **drawing out** the speech for half an hour; a few words would have done.*
- *I was really looking forward to the wedding and thought I was going to be in my element, but it turned out to be a long, **drawn-out** affair.*

iii.   (To get something out of someone--*see Practical Everyday English, page 124, the note to meaning vi*)
Example:
- *We can't let this cocky fool get away with it. We'll have to **draw** the truth **out** of him somehow.*

iv.   (To encourage someone to be less shy/more sociable--*often used with "out of his shell"*)
Example:
- *It was a real eye-opener; I saw that once you **draw him out (of his shell)** he can be quite outgoing.*

To keep a low profile   (To behave in a way that does not attract attention to oneself, i.e. to remain unnoticed)

Examples:
- *The boss has definitely got it in for you this week. If I were you, I'd **keep a low profile** for the time being.*
- *As I'm most likely to be made the scapegoat, I'm going **to keep a low profile** until everything is sorted out.*

To be outnumbered (To be in a minority--*note the active form of the verb, "to outnumber", means to be in a majority*)

Examples:
- *Even though our soldiers were heavily **outnumbered,** they put up a brave fight.*
- *The gist of what the minister was saying was that in twenty years' time we will be **outnumbered** by immigrants. Deep down, all his colleagues know he is right, but want to keep their views strictly off the record.*
- *Apparently, women **outnumber** men in this college by three to one. My son wants to apply.*

*"I could have done without him **drawing out** the speech for half an hour; a few words would have done."*

(see page 20)

Lesson Two

To shrug off

i.   (Not to be affected by criticism or failure, to deal with problems as though they do not really exist--*note the verb "**to shrug**", which means to raise one's shoulders. It usually expresses the feeling that one does not care or know about something*)
Examples:
- *He's been turned down by five universities, but each time he just picks himself up, **shrugs** it **off** and gets on with the next application.*
- *He comes across as the sort of person who **shrugs off** criticism, but deep down he gets quite put out by some of the things people come out with about his work.*
- *When she was told she had missed out on a great opportunity, she just **shrugged** her shoulders.*

ii.   (To recover quickly from/To get rid of a minor illness or infection)
Example:
- Mother to son:
  M: *Your sister was asking after you yesterday.*
  S: *Did you tell her that I still haven't managed to **shrug off** the cold I caught when her dreadful kids drenched me with the garden hose?*

A foregone conclusion (Something which is certain to happen/taken for granted--*see Practical Everyday English, page 53)*

Examples:
- *Before the interview I thought it was a **foregone conclusion** that they would take her on. However, she must have had an off-day.*
- Football fan:
  *Once in a blue moon we get through to the second round, but generally it's a **foregone conclusion** that we're going to get beaten.*

Down-to-earth (Genuine, unpretentious, practical, realistic)

Examples:
- *Jane tends to go a bit over the top with her designs; mind you, as a person she's very **down-to-earth**.*
- *Even though he is one of the richest men in the country, he's very **down-to-earth** and likes to keep a low profile.*

To blow over (To be of less significance, to be forgotten about - an argument, disagreement, scandal)

Examples:

- *I kept a low profile until the row **blew over**, but he's still got it in for me.*
- *We fell out with each other over the way he went round spreading rumours about me; but that has all **blown over** now.*

To jump/climb on the bandwagon (To do or say the same thing as many others, without having thought about it for oneself or just because it is fashionable)

Examples:
- *I'm not going to **jump on the bandwagon** and slate the play like other critics. Once it got going, it was fun.*
- *I didn't think he had it in him to make up his own mind; he usually just **climbs on the bandwagon**.*

To boil/come down to (To be the most important thing, the main point, after considering everything else)

Examples:
- A: *It's no good shrugging your shoulders as if you don't care.*
  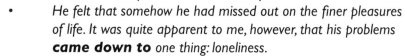
  B: *Of course I do, but you don't seem to realise that high principles and morals will have no effect on the outcome. In the end, it'll all **boil down** to who can come up with the most money.*
- *He felt that somehow he had missed out on the finer pleasures of life. It was quite apparent to me, however, that his problems **came down to** one thing: loneliness.*

To comply with (To obey, to be acceptable according to a law/ regulations)

Examples:
- Even though the judge made it very clear to the defendant that he had not **complied with** the law, he decided to let him off this time because he had so many other things on his plate. However, he was warned not to continue to go around making a nuisance of himself.
- There's a rumour going around Parliament that if we don't make an effort to **comply with** EU regulations, we will miss out when it comes to increased funds for the welfare of our run-down cities.

To nip it/something in the bud (To deal with a problem at an early stage before it gets out of hand)

Examples:
- The gist of what she was saying was that we'd be better-off **nipping it in the bud** now, rather than letting the problem grow as time goes by.
- The doctor seems to be baffled by my aunt's illness but has advised her, rather surprisingly, to **nip the whole thing in the bud** by going through with the operation.

*"He felt that somehow he had missed out on the finer pleasures of life. It was quite apparent to me, however, that his problems **came down to** one thing: loneliness."*

(see page 23)

By no/any stretch of the imagination
(In no way, definitely not-
-note that with "by no stretch of the imagination", the subject and verb are inverted–see the first
two examples below)

Examples:
- With a little brushing up, I should be able to get by in French, but **by no stretch of the imagination** <u>will I</u> ever be fluent.
- **By no stretch of the imagination** <u>could it</u> be said that the result is a foregone conclusion. There's a lot at stake for everyone involved.

- Once in a blue moon we splash out on a fine meal at a posh restaurant, but we're not wealthy **by any stretch of the imagination.**

To draw in

i. (To attract a large number of people or a lot of business)
Examples:
- What a turnout! I knew he was up and coming but I never expected him to **draw** these sorts of crowds **in**.
- He claims that he **draws in** over half of the company's turnover, but I would take everything he says with a pinch of salt.

ii. (To become night-time earlier)
Example:
- My grandmother could do without having to get round by bus, especially at this time of the year when the nights are **drawing in.**

iii. (To arrive - train or ship)
Examples

- As the train **drew into** the station, I tried to wipe out the memory I had of the last time she turned up out the blue.

iv. (To get someone involved in an argument or conversation)
Examples:
- Don't **draw me into** your rows! It serves you right if you rub everyone up the wrong way.
- Even though I tried my best to **draw her into** every conversation, she steered clear of everyone, preferring to keep a low profile.

L e s s o n   T h r e e

To sulk (To become miserable and refuse to talk to people because one has been told off/unsuccessful/not been allowed to get one's own way --*see Practical Everyday English, page 165. "To sulk" is generally used for a child or childish behaviour. Also note the use of the noun "sulk"; see third example below*)

Examples:
- *Even though the whole thing blew over ages ago, he is still **sulking** about it.*
- *I know there's a lot at stake, but if you **sulk** every time a deal doesn't come off, you're bound to miss out on the next opportunity that comes along.*
- *She's having a **sulk** because her request to take an extra day off was turned down.*

A stumbling block (An obstacle, something which/someone who prevents progress--*note that "**to stumble**" means to trip, to walk unsteadily; see third example below*)

Examples:
- *You'll get on in this company if you know how to go about avoiding the **stumbling blocks**.*
- *I don't know why she takes it out on her mother. I put all her unhappiness down to her father, who has been the main **stumbling block** in her life.*
- *I **stumbled** as I got up; that wine must have gone straight to my head.*

To come to light (To be revealed, to become clear to everyone--*note the expression "**in the light of**", which means considering, in view of. It is often used when one makes a decision based on information which has recently become known, or something which is happening at the time. The article "the" is often dropped*)

Examples:
- *When this latest piece of evidence **came to light**, he had no choice but to own up. It is quite apparent that he had not complied with the task that was set him.*
- *It has just **come to light** that this supposedly easy-going, laid-back guy is a lethal killer. Even the police didn't believe he had it in him to commit such horrendous crimes.*

In (the) light of recent events, the management has decided to call off the Christmas festivities for this year. We apologise if this has put anyone out, and we promise to keep you posted if there is any change of plan.

To lay on   (To provide a service --*often relating to food or transport,* to put on--*see Practical Everyday English, page 172, meaning vi*)

Examples:
- These meetings tend to be rather drawn-out; mind you, they always **lay on** a wonderful dinner.
- The Rolling Stones concert drew in so many people that they had to **lay on** three extra trains.

To warrant

i.   (To guarantee)
Example:
- The document your own lawyer prepared clearly **warrants** that if there are any stumbling blocks, it's up to you to sort them out.

ii.   (To call for--*see "**uncalled for**", Practical Everyday English, page 107*--to make something necessary, i.e. an action)
Examples:
- Everyone thought that his guilt was a foregone conclusion, but, as it turned out, the evidence they had to go on didn't **warrant** his arrest.
- It's no good just sitting there and sulking; the situation is so serious as to **warrant** a relentless investigation.

To write off

i.   (To accept that a debt/loss is never going to be repaid/recovered)
Examples:
- I can't get over how we managed to break even, considering how many debts we had to **write off**.
- During the slump we had to **write off** the fortune we had laid out to many of our borrowers who had not managed to come through the recession.

ii. (To accept that an idea or plan has to be scrapped--see Practical Everyday English, page 130)

Example:

- *The layout of the building we had envisaged had to be **written off** because it didn't comply with local planning regulations.*

iii. (To decide that someone/something is not worth considering or has little value, to disregard someone)

Examples:

- *At school he was **written off** as a "no-hoper". However, in later years, and much to his credit, he managed to shrug off this negative description and stand out as a brilliant journalist.*
- *Football commentator:*
  *I wouldn't **write him off** just yet. He might be getting on a bit but he can still baffle defenders with his clever tricks.*

iv. (To write a letter with a view to getting some information, goods, application forms etc.)

Example:

- *It sounds like the person who is taken on is going to be the dogsbody of the office; but you might as well **write off** <u>for</u> an application form.*

v. (To damage a motor vehicle beyond repair--note the noun "**write-off**")

Examples:

- *Father to son:*
  *Now that you've **written off** two of the family's cars, you'll have to put up with the hardship of using public transport.*
- *She got off with a broken wrist, but the car was a complete **write-off**.*

A wimp (A person who is physically or emotionally weak/lacking in confidence/always afraid) **Colloquial**

Examples:

- *Off the record, the Prime Minister owned up to being a bit of a **wimp**.*
- A: *I think we're going to be outnumbered by women at this meeting tomorrow. I'm really scared.*
  B: *Don't be such a **wimp**! I'm sure we'll cope.*

The final/last straw (A negative event, possibly minor, which comes after a series of many other negative events, and which then leads to action being taken; the situation can no longer be tolerated)

Examples:
- When the secret "goings-on" of the Managing Director came to light, that was **the final straw;** I had to give in my notice.
- At the time, I felt his inappropriate behaviour was **the last straw**, but fortunately it has all blown over now and, I'm delighted to say, our relationship has really got going again.

A: "I think we're going to be outnumbered by women at this meeting tomorrow. I'm really scared".

B: "Don't be such a **wimp**! I'm sure we'll cope."

(see page 28)

To weigh up

i. (To balance/To consider all aspects of a situation before coming to a decision)

Examples:
- *Having **weighed everything up**, we thought we'd be better off keeping a low profile.*

- *What you have to **weigh up** in your mind is whether it's worth going along with them for the time being on this one issue, or nipping the whole thing in the bud now, before you get down to business.*

ii. (To assess someone so that one can have a good idea of what type of opposition the person is likely to be)

Examples:
- *We should try to **weigh them up** beforehand, just to see precisely what we are letting ourselves in for. Let's hope their cockiness is unwarranted.*
- *Before the boxing match got under way, the two fighters carefully **weighed each other up**, but the bigger guy wrote his opponent off as being a wimp.*

PERSONAL NOTE IN DIARY

Monday 12th September

I was called into the boss's office this morning. He gave me a long drawn-out speech, the gist of which was that my work had not been up to scratch. He said that he knew that I had a lot on my plate, but it was better to nip things in the bud now. What it boiled down to was that my promotion was by no stretch of the imagination a foregone conclusion, and that my job was at stake. I can usually shrug off such criticism but I thought my boss had gone over the top. I don't feel his comments were warranted at all. Maybe I shouldn't let myself get so worried about things, but deep down, I know something isn't right. I spent the rest of the day in a sulk. What a wimp!

Tuesday 13th September

Today the company laid on a huge lunch for some clients. I could see their director was trying to weigh me up by asking me questions like, "What if a major stumbling block comes to light?" I suppose, in a way, he was quite down-to-earth, but I felt outnumbered by serious businessmen, and all I wanted to do was to keep a low profile. I got the distinct impression that in the end they wrote me off as the sort of guy who would jump on the bandwagon rather than get drawn into controversy.

A CONVERSATION BETWEEN TWO BEST FRIENDS AT LUNCH

JANE: I think I might've fallen out with my sister.

PATRICIA: Really? Why?

JANE: Well, I wrote off her car last week. We'd already had a row earlier in the day, and then I asked if I could borrow her car to pick up the kids from school. Unfortunately, I crashed into the front wall of her house. It was the final straw.

PATRICIA: Surely not? It'll all blow over in time, you'll see. Why don't you come out with us tonight? By staying at home you could be missing out on a great opportunity to meet new blokes. You only go out once in a blue moon.

JANE: Well as far as meeting a new man is concerned, at forty-three, I think I've missed the boat, and I must say, as the nights are drawing in, I can't really be bothered to go out. Sorry.

Chapter Two: **Exercise**

CHOOSE THE CORRECT WORD FROM THOSE IN RED
Answers on page 133

1. a(Down-to-earth/Deep down/Boiled down/The gist) *I knew, even before these facts* b(shrugged off/blew over/drew in/came to light), *that he hadn't been* c(complying with/asking after/nipping in the bud/jumping on the bandwagon with) *the regulations..*

2. *There's no need to* a(miss the boat/blow over/sulk/draw it out) *just because you lost a tennis match to the class* b(cocky/gist/wimp/last straw).

3. *Mum was* a(missing out/asking after/writing off/weighing up) *you yesterday. She does realise that you* b(have a lot on your plate/missed the boat/nipped it in the bud/have been outnumbered) *at the moment.*

4. *The* a(stumbling block/warrant/gist/last straw) *of what he was saying is that if we* b(miss the boat/boil it down/write it off/nip it in the bud) *now, we will be in a better position to deal with any* c(stumbling blocks/foregone conclusions/blue moons/low profiles) *that may arise later on.*

5. a(By no stretch of the imagination/Deep down/Weighing everything up/Keeping a low profile) *could it be said that it was an amazing concert. Mind you, you did* b(blow over/go over the top/jump on the bandwagon/miss out on) *seeing a fantastic drummer.*

6. *When she* a(laid on/wrote off/blew over/missed out on) *my beloved car, it was the* b(final straw/gist/warrant/foregone conclusion). After c(asking after everyone/laying everything on/weighing everything up/having a lot on my plate), *I decided to go back home and live with my parents.*

7. a(By no stretch of the imagination/Once in a blue moon/Keeping a low profile/Deep down) *we win a match on penalties, but it all* b(complies with/lays on/boils down/blows over) *to luck in the end.*

8. *Even though he's worth millions, he's a very* a(down-to-earth/over-the-top/drawn-out/cocky) *guy who likes to* b(shrug it off/nip it in the bud/miss the boat/keep a low profile).

9. *Our lecturer painfully* a(drew in/drew out/weighed up/missed out) *the seminar to two hours. We told him what we thought of this, but he just* b(complied with it/laid it on/shrugged it off/blew it over) *with a smile.*

10. *My wife and I thought that, as we lived on an island where men are* a(outnumbered/blown over/missed out/drawn in) *by women 10 to 1, our 31-year-old daughter, Sara, would more than likely* b(climb on the bandwagon/weigh it up/come to light/miss the boat). *Fortunately, our fears were not* c(outnumbered/warranted/down-to-earth/a foregone conclusion), *as she got married last year…to Monica!*

11. *As the nights are* ^a*(drawing out/blowing over/drawing in/missing out), we have decided to* ^b*(lay on/comply with/write off/shrug off) extra buses and trains so that everyone can get home quickly and safely.*

12. *It's a* ^a*(stumbling block/foregone conclusion/last straw/missed boat) that we are all going to end up rowing with each other this holiday. Mum will go totally* ^b*(on the last straw /low profile/drawn-out/over the top), as she always does. But it will all* ^c*(blow over/ask after/be up in the air/weigh up) by the time we go home.*

13. *These days in London everybody seems to be* ^a*(missing the boat/nipping it in the bud/ jumping on the bandwagon/getting touchy) and opening a shop selling gone-off fruit and ridiculously expensive tiny pieces of dry cake. You can see that this is not my favourite city* ^b*(being outnumbered/by any stretch of the imagination/keeping a low profile/deep down).*

Lesson One

To play down (To claim publicly that something is not important, even if in reality it is)

Examples:
- *The Prime Minister tried to **play down** the results of the public enquiry into pension frauds, shrugging off blame from journalists for having handled the matter incompetently.*
- *We shouldn't let ourselves get carried away over the information which has just come to light. Let's **play it down** for the time being.*

*"The Prime Minister tried to **play down** the results of the public enquiry into pension frauds, shrugging off blame from journalists for having handled the matter incompetently"*

To budge (To move something/To be moved with difficulty from its position, to change one's mind, to compromise--*often used in the negative. Note also the colloquial expression "**to budge up**", which is used to ask a person/people to make more space so that someone else can sit down*)

Examples:
- *She was the only one who managed to **budge** the fridge. I never knew she had that sort of strength in her.*
- *I know you think I'm a wimp but I'm telling you, this piano won't **budge**. You have a go!*

- *The leaders of these three European countries have told the press that they are <u>not</u> going to **budge** on their recent decision not to write off any of the Third World debt.*
- *You two kids are taking up three spaces. **Budge up** and let this lady have a seat…and stop sulking!*

To take someone's word for it (To accept/To rely on something someone says as being true or a fact, without verifying it for oneself)

Examples:
- *She assured me that the accommodation was spotless and that my client would be missing out on something if he didn't take it up. The biggest mistake I made was that I **took her word for it**. It was filthy!*
- *Don't **take my word for it**. If you don't think there'll be enough to go around, order some more…but don't go over the top.*

Prudish (Very conservative, not open-minded in respect of sexual matters--*note that a "prude" is a person who is embarrassed by sexual matters*)

Examples:
- Husband to wife:
  - H: *I don't want to jump on the bandwagon but I think these documentaries about sex for the over 40s should be frowned upon.*
  - W: *Don't be so **prudish**! We could do with more television like this.*
- *It's true that my dad is a bit of a **prude**, but he hasn't got it in him to stop my sister going out in a short skirt. He just sulks in the corner of the room not talking to my mum.*

To enlighten (To reveal information to someone who is likely to find it interesting/useful--*note also the adjective "enlightening", which means revealing/an eye-opener--see Practical Everyday English, page 186*)

Examples:
- *We got the gist of what he was on about, but perhaps you could **enlighten** us a little further on this matter.*
- *Once in a blue moon, when there's nothing much at stake, he gives us some information which is quite **enlightening**.*
- *'**Enlightening**' would be an understatement to describe the stories that went round about her family.*

To clutch at straws (To be desperate to achieve something when there is clearly little hope of success, to try to answer a question or deal with a problem, making it obvious that one has no idea what the answer is or how to deal with it)

Examples:
- A: *How is your son coping with his redundancy?*
  B: *Well, he's trying to play it down at the moment but he has been going for high level jobs in the City, even though, deep down, he knows he is just* ***clutching at straws***.
- *The Government haven't got a clue as to how to go about sorting this mess out. It's quite apparent to everyone that they're* ***clutching at straws***.

To stick something out

i.   (To continue doing something even though it is unpleasant--*note also the expression "**to stick out like a sore thumb**", which means to be noticed as being different from all the others--see also "**the odd one out**", Practical Everyday English, page 75, note to meaning v*)
Examples:
- *Take my word for it; if you weigh up all your options, you'll see that you'd be better off* ***sticking*** *your course* ***out*** *until you've qualified.*
- *I* ***stuck*** *his lessons* ***out***, *until he turned up one morning drunk. That was the final straw. I couldn't cope with him after that.*
- *He's more cocky and outgoing than his brothers and sisters. This is why he* ***sticks out like a sore thumb*** *at family gatherings.*

ii. (To be showing/visible --*often used for clothes which should be "tucked in", e.g. shirt or label*)
Examples:
- *My mother-in-law wrote me off as a scruff when I first met her because not only did I have my shirt* ***sticking out*** *(which she tucked in for me), but my shoelaces were undone, and I had odd socks on.*
- *I don't want to keep picking you up on your appearance, but did you realise the label of your pullover is* ***sticking out***?

To stick one's neck out (Not to be afraid to say what one really thinks will happen, knowing that one may later be proved to be wrong or get into trouble for saying it)

Examples:
- A: *I've bet £15 on Italy for the next World Cup. Who do you reckon's going to win it?*

  B: *It'll all boil down to which team has the fewest injuries. I'm going to **stick my neck out** and go for England.*

  A: *Ha Ha! They might have a few stumbling blocks... like the fact they aren't very good.*
- *At the meeting I had with the Managing Director yesterday I decided that, in the long run, I'd be better off **sticking my neck out** and being honest, rather than clutching at straws and coming out with something I don't really believe in. So I told him that we'd have to lay off half the workforce if we wanted to break even next year.*

To disrupt (To prevent someone from continuing with what they were doing, to spoil an occasion or event etc. by causing a disturbance--*note also the adjective "disruptive", which means causing a disturbance*)

Examples:
- *Sorry to **disrupt** you in your work, but I just wanted to tell you that I've pencilled you in for a meeting with James Reid for next Tuesday at 1.30pm. I know you have a lot on your plate, so please let me know if you can make it.*
- *He used to put up with his aunt's odd behaviour, putting it down to eccentricity; but she really rubbed him up the wrong way when she **disrupted** his wedding celebrations, and that was the final straw.*
- *We really don't know how to go about dealing with this child. Even though he is one of the brightest pupils in the class, he continues to be a **disruptive** influence on the other children.*

To be lulled into a false sense of security (To be deceived into thinking or to take for granted that, due to recent success, everything is going to be fine, when it isn't)

Examples:
- Manager of football team to his players:

  *Just because we've got through to the quarter finals without conceding a goal, I don't want you all to **be lulled into a false sense of security** and write off all the other teams left in the competition.*

- *The soldiers had thought that it was a foregone conclusion that they would outnumber the enemy. However, it later became apparent that they had **been lulled into a false sense of security**.*

To waffle (on) (To digress, to talk a lot without saying anything of significance--*note the noun "**waffle**", which means irrelevant, superficial language*)

Examples:
- *We got the gist of what he was getting at after just a couple of minutes, but then he **waffled on**, drawing out his speech for almost an hour.*
- Teacher to students:
  *Most students who fail the exam do so because instead of sticking to the task in hand, they **waffle (on)**, consequently bogging the examiner down with too much useless information.*
- *As usual, he came out with a lot of **waffle** about how the Government had come up against a few minor stumbling blocks, but that now economic recovery had got well under way.*

Lesson Two

To grow out of (To change one's taste or behaviour as one becomes more mature/ an adult)

Examples:
- *He was most disruptive as a child but fortunately he **grew out of** it.*
- *My sister dreads the idea of missing out on up-and-coming trends in music, but I **grew out of** all that nonsense quite a while ago.*

To go/come in phases (To occur at irregular intervals-e.g. business success, popularity, the desire to do/have something--*note that a "**phase**" is a temporary stage or period of time, often in a person's life or development*)

Examples:
- *Business tends to **go in phases;** for example, last week we didn't have enough work to go round the office. This week, however, we've taken on more than we can handle.*
- *My passion for Indian food **comes in phases**; sometimes I'll go over the top and eat it five nights in a row, then I'll completely go off it for a month.*
- *Doctor to parent: Your child is going through a disruptive **phase**, but I'm sure he'll grow out of it within a few months.*

Outlook

i. (General attitude towards life)
Examples:
- *He no longer sulks, but by no stretch of the imagination can it be said that he has a positive **outlook** <u>on</u> life.*
- *As he went through his old diaries, it dawned on him how much his **outlook** had changed as the years had gone by.*

ii. (Prospects, the likelihood of something getting better or worse--*often used for the economic situation or weather*)
Examples:
- *Politicians are predicting an upturn in the economy, but I'm not taking their word for it. Weighing everything up, the **outlook** is far less promising.*

- Weather forecaster:
  *The **outlook** for the weekend is quite bright, apart from patchy fog in the North. We'll keep you posted with any changes.*

Cumbersome (Large and heavy and therefore difficult to move or carry, a clumsy and heavy style of writing, slow and inefficient because of its large size and bureaucratic nature-e.g. a large company or government organisation)

Examples:
- *I don't know what came over us when we bought such a **cumbersome** wardrobe. Now, no one can get it to budge.*
- Teacher to student:
  *You tend to waffle a lot in your compositions and your style is too **cumbersome**. Try to cut down on the words you use, and then your message will come over much more effectively.*
- *It's a foregone conclusion that they won't be able to comply with EU regulations; their local government structure is far too **cumbersome**.*

To make ends meet (To earn enough money to survive or pay one's bills)

Examples:
- *He somewhat cockily makes out that they're quite well off, but I happen to know they've got through all their savings and are struggling to **make ends meet**.*
- Father to son:
  *F: When your mother and I got married, we could barely **make ends meet**, let alone go off around the world.*
  S: So you keep telling me; but I don't want to miss out on what could be a very enlightening trip.

Tactful (Careful what one says so as to avoid upsetting someone--*note the opposite of "**tactful**" is "tactless", i.e. not careful about what one says*)

Examples:
- *I think he has an uninviting, cumbersome style of writing in his books, which I find unreadable...but it wouldn't be very **tactful** of me to tell him.*

- A: *I think it would be more **tactful** of you if you didn't bring it up until the whole thing has blown over.*
- B: *No, I'm sorry; I reckon we'll all be better off if the matter is nipped in the bud right now.*
- *I can't get over how **tactless** you are sometimes. Fancy telling her she was only taken on as a dogsbody.*

To butt in (To interrupt a conversation)

Examples:
- *Sorry to **butt in**, but I just wanted to tell you that I'm popping out to get some tea bags. Apparently, there aren't enough to go round.*
- Parent to child:
  *Stop sulking! I only told you off because you should know how rude it is to **butt in** when I'm talking to someone.*

Teacher to student:
*"You tend to waffle a lot in your compositions and your style is too **cumbersome**. Try to cut down on the words you use, and then your message will come over much more effectively."*

(see page 40)

To stand one in good stead (To be or have been a good preparation for the future, even if the experience seems unpleasant at the time, to be of good service to one, i.e. an object)

Examples:
- *Looking back, it is only just beginning to dawn on me how my childhood hardships **stood me in good stead** later on in life. It's a wonder I ever came through it all.*
- *This handy computer will **stand you in good stead** when you've got a backlog of work to get through.*

I wouldn't put it past him/her ("It wouldn't surprise me if he/she did a thing like that"--*usually expressed in a negative sense*)

Examples:
- A: *Do you think he's likely to disrupt the meeting again with the same outrageous behaviour?*
- B: ***I wouldn't put it past him**!*
- *I **wouldn't put it past her** to use him as a scapegoat. Alternatively, as there's so much at stake, she might decide to play the whole thing down.*

Uneasy (Unsure, fearful, nervous, anxious--*note the noun "**uneasiness**", i.e. anxiety or fear*)

Examples:
- *They were a little **uneasy** about taking him on because he came over as rather cocky in the interview but, as it turned out, his down-to-earth approach towards sorting out problems has gone down well with their clients.*
- *We felt **uneasy** about our daughter going to all-night parties. Fortunately, as the years went by, we realised it was just a phase which she would grow out of.*
- *When this most recent piece of information came to light, we realised that our **uneasiness** had been warranted.*

Lesson Three

To bring out

i.   (To produce, publish something, i.e. book, CD etc.)
Examples:
- A: *I'm baffled as to why he didn't **bring out** this book much earlier.*

  B: *Perhaps he felt it might rub certain people up the wrong way.*
- *Apparently, they have a backlog of about a hundred previously unreleased songs of his which they hope to **bring out** this Christmas.*

ii.   (To encourage someone to be less shy, to draw out--*see Chapter 2, page 20*)
Example:
- *It's really quite enlightening. Who would have guessed that your prudish mother would be the only one who could **bring her out** (of her shell) and talk her into discussing her sexual problems?*

iii.   (To cause a particular type of behaviour or sentiment in someone which is not normally seen--*often used with "best" or "worst" followed by "in"*)
Examples:
- *We thought that our relationship had a lot going for it, but unfortunately it has recently dawned on us that we **bring out the worst in** each other....and that we're just clutching at straws trying to keep up appearances.*
- *His outlook on life became much more positive when the business started to get going. It really has **brought out the optimist in** him.*

iv.   (To expose the qualities of someone or something, such as a writer/composer or a piece of music/drama)
Examples:
- *I had underrated her piano playing in the past but now I realise what I was missing out on: she **brings out** Mozart's subtlety beautifully.*
- *The actors seemed to shrug off the criticism that they had failed to **bring out** the play's humour; mind you, a couple of them were clearly put out by the fact that it had not received a single rave review.*

By and large (Mostly/On the whole)

Examples:
- **By and large**, the people in this town can make ends meet, but the outlook is quite depressing.
- We have, **by and large**, achieved our financial targets for this year but we mustn't allow ourselves to be lulled into a false sense of security.

Bland (Without character or flavour, superficial, unexciting--*especially food or music*)

Examples:
- When I was pregnant, I couldn't handle spicy food. I usually stuck to **bland** yoghurts and pasta, which were hardly exciting by any stretch of the imagination.
- My brother grew out of heavy rock music in his twenties. Since then he has gone for a much **blander** sound and his friends have written him off as an old bore.

To corner the market (To dominate/Take control of a certain market so that one's competitors have little chance of success in this field)

Examples:
- I'm going to stick my neck out here and say that if we go through with these plans, we will have **cornered** the entire computer software **market** by this time next year.
- After our product line had undergone a complete change of design, we thought we would **corner the market**. We didn't know what we were letting ourselves in for at the time, and now looking back, we should have weighed up our options more thoroughly.

Complacent (Too satisfied with oneself so that one has a feeling that it is not necessary to try to improve, make an effort or worry about anything--*note the noun "complacency"*)

Examples:
- This year's turnover is the best we've ever had but we can't afford to be **complacent**; there's too much at stake.
- Since he has been top of the class, he has become **complacent** about his exams. I think he's going about them in the wrong way.
- We won't stand for **complacency** in this firm. Don't for one moment think that your promotion is a foregone conclusion.

To turn off

i.   (To switch off the supply of electricity, water or gas)
    Example:
- *Don't you think you should **turn** the TV **off** and get on with some work? These bland game shows bring out your lazy streak.*

ii.   (To take a road going away from the main road which one is travelling along)
    Examples
- *I'm baffled as to why Dad always **turns off** here. Surely he'd be better off going straight on and dodging the hold-ups on the A3?*

iii.   (To disgust someone, to make someone feel uninterested--*especially in a sexual sense–note the noun "**turn-off**" and see Practical Everyday English, page 160 for the opposite "**to turn on**" and the noun "**turn-on**"*)
    Examples:
- Wife to husband:
  *Do you know that it really **turns me off** when I see you biting your nails? I thought you would have grown out of that childish habit by now.*
- A: *He'll probably come out with some nonsense about marriage being a **turn-off**.*
  B: *I wouldn't put it past him!*

To be the laughing stock (To be the person, team, country etc. whom everyone makes fun of/laughs at--*especially when he/it has previously been considered to be the best or very important*)

    Examples:
- *If you go by what the experts are saying, the outlook for English tennis is not very promising. We have been the **laughing stock** of world tennis for far too long.*
- *As a young actor it was reckoned that he had a lot going for him and was apparently highly sought-after. However, the goings-on which have recently come to light have made him the **laughing stock** of the theatre.*

To bear in mind (To consider or note, not to forget about a certain fact or person)

Examples:
- *I know she has been a bit touchy lately, but you have to* **bear in mind** *what she's been through during the last year.*
- *He came in for a lot of stick over the way he handled his personal life, but the directors have promised they will* **bear him in mind** *when the position of Vice Chairman comes up at the end of the year.*

Streetwise (Used to describe a person who, through experience, has become aware of the dangers and risks of life/business/people who should not be trusted)

Examples:
- *Saying my brother isn't* **streetwise** *is an understatement. Any fool could take him in.*
- A: *Survival in this city boils down to how* **streetwise** *you are.*

  B: *I'll vouch for that!*

To touch on (To mention something only briefly)

Examples:
- *I'd like to pick up on some of the points we* **touched on** *last time. I know many of you feel uneasy about this subject, but it's not something that's just going to blow over.*
- *The Prime Minister refused to be put on the spot and just* **touched on** *the matter, assuring the journalists present that plans were in the pipeline to get the road-building work going as soon as possible.*

*"Saying my brother isn't **streetwise** is an understatement. Any fool could take him in."*

(see page 46)

If you haven't experienced the joys of bringing up teenagers, take my word for it, it brings out the worst in you. By and large, I would say I'm quite an easy-going person by nature, but a lively, disruptive child can make me feel uneasy. I once read a book about bringing up boys and I must say I found it most enlightening. It says that the vast majority of kids grow out of their annoying habits and that their periods of awkwardness come in phases. The outlook, apparently, is positive for caring, worried parents. It is clear that what you can teach children early on in life will stand them in good stead for the future.

However, you have to be tactful when giving advice to teenagers, and in particular be careful not to waffle on about the dangers of sex. They would just think you were being prudish.

Many times you think your son is not going to budge over a certain issue, but if you play down the matter, he will think you are just being complacent. The thing to do is stick it out. You'll get your own way in the end. I always say I wouldn't put it past my son to leave home and never speak to me again…but he'd soon come back after finding he couldn't make ends meet.

INTERVIEWER: *Is it true you've changed the direction of your music because you felt that you stuck out like a sore thumb in the classical musical world?*

MUSICIAN: *In part, yes because I found out that…*

INTERVIEWER: *Sorry to butt in, but you are on record as saying that the people you were working with were often stuck-up, and that you were also getting fed up having to carry around a huge cumbersome double bass.*

MUSICIAN: *Yes all very true…although a lot of what you say is taken out of context. But apart from that, I felt there were other musicians who had cornered the classical market, and so I was persuaded by my producer to bring out something more down-to-earth.*

INTERVIEWER: *If you don't mind me saying, people have said it's bland and that you have become the laughing stock of the classical world.*

MUSICIAN: *That's their opinion. What is definitely true is that I've become more streetwise. You have to bear in mind that most people from my musical background haven't got a clue about what's going on in the world. They turn off the news when anything political comes up. Their lives are far too comfortable. I don't want to be lulled into the same false sense of security. I hope you get the gist of what I'm saying…but I don't want to come over as being pretentious.*

INTERVIEWER: *Not at all, and thank you. I wish you all the best with your new CD.*

Chapter Three: **Exercise**

CHOOSE THE CORRECT WORD FROM THOSE IN RED
Answers on page 133

1.   *Please feel free to* ª(budge up/disrupt/stick out/butt in) *if you think I'm* ᵇ(waffling on/playing down/cornering the market/touching on) *for too long.*

2.   *When he lost his job two years ago, he found it hard to* ª(be disruptive/make ends meet/clutch at straws/bear it in mind), *but,* ᵇ(by and large/complacently/uneasily/playing it down), *that difficult period has* ᶜ(turned him off/come in phases/stood him in good stead/grown out of him)*in recent times.*

3.   *The new teacher felt a bit* ª(bland/uneasy/prudish/streetwise) *about taking over such a* ᵇ(complacent/turned off/disruptive/cumbersome) *class, but by the end of term, she felt she had managed to* ᶜ(budge/bring out the best/enlighten/butt) *in them.*

4.   *A: I told Maria that I thought her cooking was a bit* ª(uneasy/complacent/cumbersome/bland).
     B: That wasn't very ᵇ(tactful/uneasy/disruptive/prudish) *of you, was it?*

5.   *I don't know how you think you're going to* ª(stand in good stead/corner the market/stick out like a sore thumb/clutch at straws)*with such an expensive product. You have to* ᵇ(bear in mind/enlighten/budge up/play down) *that the economic* ᶜ(unease/prude/outlook/market) *is not very positive at the moment, and people aren't splashing out.*

6.   *We mustn't let our recent success* ª(touch on us/lull us into a false sense of security/budge us up/disrupt us). *I'm sure you are all aware how dangerous* ᵇ(clutching at straws/sticking out like a sore thumb/streetwise/complacency) *can be.*

7.   *He likes to* ª(play down/stick out/butt in/turn off) *his celebrity status as a TV historian, but we have all found his documentaries most* ᵇ(streetwise/bland/complacent/enlightening).

8.   *A: Do you think he realises that at the age of 52 he* ª(goes in phases/sticks out like a sore thumb/is lulled into a false sense of security/looks cumbersome) *at the university bar?*
     B: I don't think he does. He's trying to find himself a beautiful young wife. It's so sad to see him ᵇ(taking my word for it/putting it past him/clutching at straws/turning them off).

9.   *A: I have failed to convince your father that you are now old enough to wear a bikini on the beach. He won't* ª(budge/disrupt/turn off/bear it in mind)*on this matter, I'm afraid.*
     B: Why am I the only one of my friends with such a ᵇ(disruptive/streetwise/prudish/waffling) *dad?*

10. ª(Be enlightened/Take my word for it/Bear it in mind/Grow out of it)*: if we don't toughen up and get more* ᵇ(prudish/disruptive/cumbersome/streetwise), *we'll be the* ᶜ(laughing stock/outlook/complacency/enlightened) *of the business community in this city.*

11. A: *Do you think she's likely to tell him that she finds his physical appearance to be one big* [a]*(complacency/turn-off/uneasiness/prude)?*
B: *I wouldn't* [b]*(touch on it/bring it out/put it past her/take her word for it)!*

12. *Doctor, I know it's a matter you have* [a]*(stuck out/brought out/waffled on/touched on) previously, but do you really believe that David will ever* [b]*(come in phases/grow out of/bear in mind/make ends meet) his aggressive behaviour towards his younger brother?*

13. *My interest in the self-study French course I'm doing in my spare time* [a]*(comes in phases/ makes ends meet/enlightens me/brings out the best in me). But I'm going to* [b]*(disrupt it/ stick it out/touch on it/bear it in mind) until the end, whatever happens.*

Stilted (Unnatural and old-fashioned use of language--*especially in writing*)

Examples:
- Teacher to student:
  *Your project is good, in that it doesn't bog down the reader with too much information. However, some of your language is a little **stilted**.*
- *This novel is a massive, cumbersome piece of work, which didn't really get going until halfway through. I was also put off by the writer's somewhat **stilted** style of prose.*

To get to the bottom of something (To resolve a long-standing problem)

Examples:
- *We'll have to **get to the bottom of** this issue and find out why he has been made the scapegoat.*
- *Deep down, she still feels that the doctors haven't **got to the bottom** of her illness.*

Distraught (Extremely worried)

Examples:
- *She has enough on her plate with her husband's health. This latest piece of news must have made her even more **distraught.***
- *'**Distraught**' is an understatement as to how we felt when our daughter told us she will be travelling through Africa alone next year during her 'gap' year. She's clearly just jumped on the bandwagon to follow what so many young people in the UK do before going to university…without thinking it through properly.*

To get flustered (To get into a state of panic or nervousness)

Examples:
- *Even though she's outgoing and confident, she gets too easily **flustered** when she comes up against the tiniest problem at work.*

- *Despite being put on the spot, the Prime Minister didn't allow himself to get **flustered** by the questions that were fired at him, and played down the current crisis.*

Passé (No longer fashionable)

Example:
- *You're on record as saying that you have a soft spot for some kinds of music considered **passé** by the youth of today.*

Squeamish (Afraid of the sight of blood, easily disgusted by unpleasant images)

Example:
- *As a surgeon I can't afford to be **squeamish**; I just take flesh and blood in my stride. Having to comply with stupid government regulations is much more of a problem for me.*
- Doctor and Patient:
  Dr: *Are you **squeamish** at all ?*
  P: *No, not really, although my friends gave me stick once for fainting after an injection.*

To get a kick out of something (To enjoy/get special pleasure out of doing something--*very often something dangerous, unusual or something most other people would not enjoy*)

Example:
- *It baffles me as to how some people **get a kick out of** breaking the law; I've always gone by the book in whatever I do.*
- *He clearly **gets a kick out of** treating people like dogsbodies. He can't continue to go round with that attitude.*

Handful

i. (A few)
Examples:
- *There are a **handful** of young players coming through at the club.*
- *I got so flustered on the nightmare car journey going to the party, worried that we'd never get there. When we did eventually arrive, there were only a **handful** of people left. But it didn't seem to me that we'd missed out on any fun.*

ii. (Difficult to deal with--*especially children*)
Examples:
- Even though her children can be quite a **handful** at times, she's a loving, affectionate mum whose kids bring out the best in her.
- He claims that his youngest son is a real **handful;** mind you, you can't always go by what he says about his children.

"Even though she's outgoing and confident, she gets too easily **flustered** when she comes up against the tiniest problem at work."

(see page 52)

To pass out (To faint)

Examples:
- If you want to rub her up the wrong way, wind her up about the time she **passed out** at the school parade. It took her at least 20 seconds to come round.
- I almost **passed out** when I saw the backlog of work I had to get through. How was I going to catch up?

Pompous (Too formal /serious and self-important)

Examples:
- What came through most of all was his **pompous** attitude towards the younger members of the firm.
- He gets a lot of stick from his kids for being a bit on the **pompous** side, but I find him very witty…although he does waffle on.

Lesson Two

To get one's comeuppance (To get the punishment one deserves)

Examples:
- *Take my word for it: one day he's going to **get his comeuppance**, and it will serve him right!*
- *He treated everyone like dogsbodies but he soon **got his comeuppance**. His new boss didn't take to his behaviour at all and gave him the sack.*

Past it (Too old to do the things young people do) **Colloquial**

Examples:
- *Just because I'm getting on a bit, it doesn't mean I'm **past it**. The tennis coaching I had as a youngster has stood me in good stead later on in life, and I'm very excited about taking you on…so don't get too complacent.*
- *My dad gets a real kick out of disco dancing. I thought he was **past it** and that watching him on the dance floor was going to make me cringe, but as it turned out, it was a real eye-opener to see what he was capable of getting up to.*

To play up

i.   (To be naughty)
Examples:
- *He's quite a cocky little boy who tends to **play up** when his parents have a lot on their plate.*
- *I usually get all flustered when other people's kids start to **play me up**.*

ii.   (Not to work properly and therefore cause a problem--*very often used for a part of the body*) **Colloquial**
Examples:
- *My hip does **play me up** from time to time, but I don't let it disrupt my day. Yesterday, however, I nearly passed out from the pain it was giving me.*
- *A: The car is **playing up** again.*
  B: You know, I think it's past it. Would it be such a hardship to go without a holiday this year and invest in a new one ?

iii. (To exaggerate, emphasise)
Examples:
- There's no point trying to **play up** your symptoms to the doctor. Bear in mind that he sees patients like you all day long, and will see through exactly what you're up to.
- A: I don't really know how to go about dealing with the problem, but I have to avoid being tactless.
  B: Something which doesn't come easily to you. You'll have to **play up** the sensitive side to your nature.

To dwell on (To think or speak about something for a long time)

Examples:
- I know you've been through a bad patch, but there's no point **dwelling on** it. We may never get to the bottom of what happened, but it will all blow over in good time. You'll see.
- I don't want to **dwell on** this subject but I'm not sure that the message has got through to you. So let me tell you one more time: you're past it!

To go astray (To go missing)

Examples:
- I was prepared to let my cleaning lady off when I lost my watch, but now two necklaces have **gone astray**. It's the final straw; she has to go.
- When he told me my letter must have **gone astray**, I took his word for it. But on reflection, I wouldn't put it past him to have hidden it somewhere.
- I do feel uneasy about letting my elderly dad live on his own. I worry he might **go astray** when out shopping and not find his way home.

Stranded (Left without the means to get home or to get around, to be stuck somewhere without means of escape)

Examples:
- One hour went by before we saw the first car; until then we were **stranded** in the middle of the countryside.
- I was very put out by your behaviour at that party. You left us **stranded** in the middle of a bunch of pompous businessmen. We were outnumbered!

To relish (To enjoy/take pleasure in something, to look forward to something--*note that we cannot always use "to relish" instead of " to enjoy". We could not, for example, say "I relished the party". It is usually used with "the thought", "prospect", "idea" or "challenge" of doing something*)

Examples:
- I don't really **relish** the thought of having to get through this backlog of paperwork.
- What came through most of all was how he **relishes** the challenge of competition.
- A: She didn't particularly **relish** the idea of being his dogsbody for the next twenty years, so she gave in her notice.

  B: But how is she going to make ends meet without a job?

"I know you've been through a bad patch, but there's no point **dwelling on** it.
We may never get to the bottom of what happened, but it will all blow over in good time. You'll see."

(see page 56)

To lose track of (To forget that it is getting late, not to know where something or someone is, to lose the thread of a story or argument)

Examples:
- A: *Sorry to butt in, but we'd better be off. It's getting on for eleven o'clock.*

  B: *So it is. I do **lose track of** time when I'm waffling on.*
- *We didn't fall out with each other; I just **lost track of** them when they moved to Manchester. John must be in his element living up there near his beloved football team.*
- A: *You'll have to fill me in on what has been going on in this TV series. I **lost track of** the story when I went on holiday last month.*

  B: *Sorry I didn't keep you posted, but you didn't miss out on much.*

To get one's head round something (To understand something complicated/a difficult situation--*often used with "can't/couldn't"*) **Colloquial**

Examples:
- *These figures from the accountant are baffling me; I <u>cannot</u> **get my head round** them at all.*
- *I <u>couldn't</u> **get my head round** what had happened and why she was feeling so distraught, but I think it may be better not to dwell on these things for too long.*

To give someone the benefit of the doubt (To accept someone's version of events…even though in reality one is not so sure that they are telling the truth)

Examples:
- *We've decided to **give you the benefit of the doubt** and let you off…but next time don't try to make someone else the scapegoat.*
- *The gist of what they were saying was that, as his whole career was at stake, this time they would **give him the benefit of the doubt**.*

Lesson Three

Amid/Amidst (Amongst, during, in the middle of)

Examples:
- *It was a foregone conclusion that **amid** the chaos last week, we would lose track of time.*
- *It is said, off the record, that **amidst** all the rumours going around about his affairs, he has also come in for a lot of stick over his business dealings.*

Unwittingly/Inadvertently (Without realising, unaware)

Examples:
- ***Unwittingly**, I left her stranded in the kitchen with a handful of very noisy children. She wasn't really in her element.*
- *I thought my wallet had gone astray but, **inadvertently**, I had left it on the table.*

To get something out of one's system (To do/say something one has always wanted to do/say, so that it is no longer on one's mind, therefore making one feel better)

Examples:
- *I had been feeling distraught at the thought of what I had to say to the boss, but now I've **got it out of my system**, I can relish the challenge of being given greater responsibility in the future.*
- *She has always wanted to travel and, once her visa comes through, she will be able to get it **out of her system**.*

Unrest (Civil disturbance--*often caused by the public's unhappiness with the economic or political state of affairs in their country*)

Example:
- *The Government have to weigh up whether or not it's worth risking civil **unrest** over such a sensitive issue.*
- *Everything seems to be up in the air at the moment, but amidst the fears of an economic downturn, there is bound to be industrial **unrest** unless the matter is resolved quickly.*

To take the mickey out of someone (To mock/tease/make fun of someone) **Slang**

Examples:
- Don't **take the mickey out of** him because you might rub him up the wrong way.
- She doesn't like people **taking the mickey out of** her dad's strong Spanish accent. She's clearly quite touchy about it.

To reap the rewards (To enjoy the benefits of something)

Examples:
- A: I relish the prospect of England winning the World Cup. I think the whole country would really **reap the rewards** afterwards.

  B: I would pass out!
- One loses track of time. I wrote the book ages ago, but have only just begun to **reap the rewards**. Many critics wrote my work off as being passé. Pompous idiots!

*"I had been feeling distraught at the thought of what I had to say to the boss, but now I've **got it out of my system**, I can relish the challenge of being given greater responsibility in the future."*

(see page 59)

To rake it in (To earn a lot of money) **Colloquial**

Examples:
- *It's true my salary has improved, but by no stretch of the imagination could you say I was **raking it in**.*
- *He used to get a lot of stick for being the office dogsbody, but now that he's **raking it in**, no one can take the mickey out of him.*

To skim the surface (To deal with a matter only superficially)

Examples:
- A: *I thought what the accountant told us this morning was most enlightening.*

  B: *Really? I felt he was just **skimming the surface**. I'm not sure if he's got to the bottom of what's going on here.*
- *You're on record as saying the Government has merely **skimmed the surface** as far as reducing hospital waiting lists is concerned, and has become rather complacent about it in recent times.*

Gobsmacked (Astonished, shocked) **Slang**

Examples:
- *We were totally **gobsmacked** when it was announced that John was to be the next captain of the rugby team. He's such a wimp. None of us can get our heads round this odd decision.*
- *'Surprised' is a gross understatement. I was absolutely **gobsmacked**. I never knew she had it in her to be so nasty.*

Like chalk and cheese (Completely different--*generally used to describe two people or things whom/which one would expect to be similar*)

Examples:
- *It's difficult to draw Sandra out of her shell, but her sister is quite outgoing. They're **like chalk and cheese**.*
- *'My mum and dad are like **chalk and cheese**. It's a wonder they have stuck married life out for so long.*

REVIEW OF DAVID JONES'S BOOK "A SUMMER TOO LATE"

It is true that of late David Jones's work has been considered *passé*. For some, the prose is too *stilted* and he tends to *dwell on* out-of-date issues. For this reason I did not particularly *relish* the prospect of new *pompous* material. However, his present book "A Summer Too Late", and his last book "Alone", about a man stranded on a Scottish island, are *like chalk and cheese*.

"A Summer Too Late" is about a *distraught* teenager whose life *goes astray* after his parents' divorce. Sometimes it's difficult to *get one's head round* the plot, and I did occasionally *lose track of the story*, but in the main, it is compelling reading. It seems, at times, that Jones is trying *to get something out of his system*. He quite clearly wants to tell us what he thinks of traditional family roles, and there is no doubt that this book will create *unrest* in the conventional literary world.

If you have not particularly enjoyed Jones's work in the past, and feel he has got away with some poor literature, it is time to *give him the benefit of the doubt*. I can only *skim the surface* of his novel in these few lines, but I think you may be pleasantly surprised.

Finally, whatever anyone feels about "A Summer Too Late", it is quite clear that, *amidst* all the controversy the book will undoubtedly create, the writer will soon be *raking it in*.

A CONVERSATION BETWEEN TWO POLICEMEN

STEVE: *You know, I'm so glad we* got to the bottom *of the Smith murder enquiry; mind you, it was obvious that the culprit was going to* get his comeuppance.

GAVIN: *Yes, the Superintendent was getting quite* flustered *towards the end, as we only had a* handful *of clues.*

STEVE: *To tell you the truth, I think he's* past it. *What's really amazing is that we did all the work, but he will* reap the rewards. *I was truly* gobsmacked *when he took all the credit for what we had done.*

GAVIN: *I was too… and have you noticed that he seems to* get a kick out of *presiding over all the nasty murders? I'm too* squeamish *myself. I would have* passed out *if I had found that body. Anyway, let's stop talking about work. Fancy a beer?*

Chapter Four: **Exercise**

CHOOSE THE CORRECT WORD FROM THOSE IN RED
Answers on page 133

1. My kids ª(dwell on/take the mickey out of/get a kick out of/lose track of) me when I'm being ᵇ(distraught/passé/pompous/squeamish) trying to impress our posh neighbours.

2. His aunt and uncle are ª(like chalk and cheese/raking it in/past it/a handful). Sheila ᵇ(reaps the rewards/gets flustered/is distraught/loses track) easily, while Derek ᶜ (dwells on/skims the surface/goes astray/relishes) leaving things until the last minute and takes everything in his stride.

3. The President has ª(squeamishly/inadvertently/handfully/pompously) caused ᵇ(unrest/ passing out/stranded/astray) amongst the citizens by introducing a set of tough laws and regulations. I fear he will get his ᶜ(rewards/chalk and cheese/comeuppance/stilted) at the next election.

4. ª(Amidst/Losing track of/Unwittingly/Gobsmackingly) all the excitement of the wedding celebrations, no-one had noticed that my mother-in-law had ᵇ(lost track/gone astray/skimmed the surface/passed out). We were all quite ᶜ(past it/distraught/stranded/ unrestful) until she came round.

5. I've ª(got a kick out of/played up/lost track/raked it in) of how many times recently I've had a go at the kids for ᵇ(reaping the rewards/playing me up/skimming the surface/going astray). They really can be quite ᶜ(a handful/passé/past it/stranded) at times.

6. It's probably best that we don't ª(go astray/skim the surface/dwell/take the mickey)on the issue and this time ᵇ(get it out of the system/give him the benefit of the doubt/reap the rewards/get flustered). He's never got into trouble before.

7. How on earth did you let so much money ª(pass out/get stranded/reap the rewards/go astray)? I just can't ᵇ(rake it in/get a kick out of/get my head round/dwell on) this massive loss of funds.

8. I really think we should try our best to ª(get to the bottom of/take the mickey out of/reap the rewards of/get a kick out of) this difficult problem rather than simply ᵇ(take the mickey/ get to the bottom of/rake it in/skim the surface).

9. I was totally ª(stranded/squeamish/pompous/gobsmacked) when he told me how much he was earning. Who would have believed when we were at school together that this wimp would now be ᵇ(passing out/raking it in/pompous/skimming the surface)?

10. This type of theatre production has been done so many times, it's considered ª(passé/ squeamish/stranded/gone astray) by all the critics. I have to say that I also find the dialogue very ᵇ(distraught/stilted/relished/gobsmacked).

11.   *When I was a kid, I used to* [a]*(get my comeuppance/reap the rewards/get my head round/ get a real kick out of) telling my little sister very bloody horror stories. It was nasty of me because I knew how* [b]*(pompous/squeamish/past it/gobsmacked) she was.*

12.   *I had always wanted to swim the English channel and felt I needed to* [a]*(give it the benefit of the doubt/get it out of my system/reap the rewards/get my comeuppance), even though my children kept telling me I was* [b]*(past it/pompous/squeamish/passé). But one night I had a bad dream, where I was left* [c]*(gobsmacked/amidst/like chalk and cheese/stranded) in the middle of a freezing cold sea with no one around to help, so I gave up on the idea.*

Chapter Five
Lesson One

To do one's head in (To drive one mad/crazy) **Slang**

Examples:
- *I hate it when the nights begin to draw in. Winter really **does my head in**.*
- *I've lost track of how many times I've given him the benefit of the doubt. Enough is enough! It's really **doing my head in**.*

To back down (To withdraw an argument or demand)

Examples:
- *Off the record, I think the sponsors are going to **back down** over how Wembley Stadium should be laid out.*
- *I really don't know how to go about getting them to **back down**. I'll just have to keep going on at them and hope the message eventually gets through.*

Fiasco (A complete failure, disaster, chaos)

Examples:
- *He got a lot of stick for the show he put on last year. It turned out to be a **fiasco**.*
- *He may be streetwise, but his poor attention to detail will soon lead to another organisational **fiasco**. Please bear this in mind next time you think of asking him to do anything.*

To get a buzz out of/from something (To get great excitement from doing something--*note if one says that a place has a "buzz", it means that it has an exciting atmosphere*) **Colloquial**

Examples:
- *I **get a real buzz** out of the business, even if we're only breaking even.*
- *I used to **get a buzz** from reading rave reviews of my plays, but then I got lulled into a false sense of security and probably became a bit too complacent. I got my comeuppance, though: my next production was a flop.*
- *I miss the **buzz** of London so much. By and large, countryside towns are so bland by comparison.*

Perpetual (Never ending--*generally negative*)

Examples:
- *It's not simply a question of getting their frustration out of their system; there seems to be **perpetual** unrest amongst the students of this college.*
- *Trying to get my head round these statistics is proving to be a **perpetual** nightmare.*

Pathetic (Awful, useless, feeble--*note the more traditional and formal meaning of "pathetic", which is used to describe someone/something which causes sympathy, makes one feel sorry--see 3rd example below*)

Examples:
- *You can't go by what the **pathetic** tabloid press comes out with. It all boils down to the fact that lies and gossip sell newspapers.*
- *I'm baffled as to how a team with players of such a high quality can put on a **pathetic** performance like that. My grandmother could have played better than those wimps!*
- *It was **pathetic** to see a man who had been through many hardships in his life struggling to make ends meet.*

It's down to you/him etc (It's your/his responsibility)

Examples:
- *I'll pencil it in for Thursday the 18th, but remember, **it's down to you** to make the arrangements.*
- *The gist of what he was saying is that the current fiasco **is down to** his mother-in-law's negative outlook on life and her unreasonable attitude. She refuses to back down.*

To bluff one's way through something (To pretend that one knows a lot about a subject--*note the expression "**to call someone's bluff**", which means to encourage someone to prove that what they are saying is true, or to do something they had been threatening to do, in the belief they will not actually do it*)

Examples:
- *It's pathetic, really, how someone of my limited knowledge of chemistry can **bluff his way** through an exam without brushing up beforehand.*
- *He's in his element when he has to **bluff his way through** a subject where he's outnumbered by people who know what they're talking about. He relishes the challenge.*

- *I don't think he's got it in him to carry his threat out. Why don't we **call his bluff** and see if he has the guts to do it?*

Adept (Skilful/Expert)

Examples:
- *He is somewhat **adept** at reaping the rewards of his actions, although his wife tries to play down his talents.*
- *She is usually an **adept** speaker. This time, however, she only managed to skim the surface of each issue.*

To wallow in (To indulge/lose oneself in pleasure, to enjoy one's own misery or misfortune)

Examples:
- *I could do with a weekend away with my husband, amid the green rolling hills of the beautiful English countryside, where we can turn off our phones and laptops and **wallow in** the sheer luxury of a manor house hotel.*
- *At the moment all she wants to do is sulk and **wallow in** self-pity. It's a phase she's going through.*

*"I've lost track of how many times I've given him the benefit of the doubt. Enough is enough! It's really **doing my head in.**"*

(see page 65)

L e s s o n   T w o

Frenzy, frenzied (Uncontrolled behaviour, wild)

Examples:
- At first there was only a small amount of unrest amongst the crowd, but this soon turned into a **frenzy** after some provocation from the government forces.
- The police are baffled as to what could have caused such a **frenzied** attack. One needs to be very streetwise these days; there are some very nasty people around.

To dwindle (To be reduced to a small number or nothing--*often used with "away"*)

Examples:
- Last year we were raking it in, but now our funds have **dwindled** <u>away</u> to nothing. But I'm not going to allow myself to dwell on it.
- Despite perpetual advertising, the number of clients has been **dwindling** in recent years. And the business has definitely lost its buzz for me.

To make a mockery of (To make something appear worthless, ridiculous)

Examples:
- He took advantage of a loophole which **made** a complete **mockery of** the law. I don't think he'll get away with it next time.
- I'll keep you posted as to how he does on the course, but if someone as thick as he is can pass, it will make a **mockery of** the exam.

Shortlist, to be shortlisted (A final list of names from which one could be selected, to be selected for a prize, a job or a university place etc.)

Examples:
- A: There's a rumour going about that he's been put on the **shortlist** for the Nobel Peace Prize.

  B: How enlightening! His armies have wiped out thousands of villages in his own country.
- He has been **shortlisted** for the position of editor. I didn't know he had it in him.

Upsurge (A rapid increase or a rise in something)

Examples:
- *There has been an **upsurge** in this type of political fiasco in recent years.*
- *The Managing Director of London Electricity has said that supply problems during the World Cup were down to a massive **upsurge** in demand.*

*"I'll keep you posted as to how he does on the course, but if someone as thick as he is can pass, it will make a **mockery of** the exam"*

(see page 68)

To phase in/out   (To introduce or get rid of a law/regulation /new system gradually, over a period of time)

Examples:
- *The Treasury minister promised that the new Government would be **phasing in** regulations to restrict banks on how much they pay their investment bankers. I wouldn't put it past him, however, to change his mind next week.*
- *Some financial journalists have predicted that Germany will be **phasing out** the Euro over the next five years. Then, it is hoped, they will reap the rewards of being able to control their own currency.*

Jaded (Tired and fed up)

Examples:

- I wish I didn't have such a backlog of paperwork to catch up on. I'm feeling **jaded** and could do with a rest.
- I think he got bogged down with too many questions and therefore his response sounded a bit **jaded**. Also, his hip has been playing him up recently, which doesn't help.

Pledge/to pledge (A promise or guarantee/to promise or guarantee --*often an amount of money or allegiance to a political cause*)

Examples:

- He has made a **pledge** to up-and-coming politicians, many of whom are already quite adept at bluffing their way through parliamentary meetings, that he will give them an opportunity to bring up any issues they wish to have clarified.
- They were made the scapegoats for the collapse of the company because many people had **pledged** their life savings to fund future projects.

Boisterous (Lively, noisy --*often used to describe the behaviour of a young person or dog*)

Examples:

- My teenage son can be quite **boisterous** and often goes over the top, but deep down I wouldn't change one bit of him.
- Once in a blue moon my dog, Jason, can be quite docile and laid-back, but much of the time he is too **boisterous** for most people to cope with.

Aftermath (A period of time and consequences which follow a disaster, accident, war or other important event)

Examples:

- In the **aftermath** of the war, the Conservatives found themselves to be heavily outnumbered by socialists in Parliament.
- During the **aftermath** of this scandal, he was advised to keep a low profile. This is what happens when you break a pledge to the citizens of this country. Support for his policies is dwindling by the day.

Lesson Three

To pre-empt (To take action in anticipation of an event, to prevent something happening--*note the word "**pre-emptive**", which is used to describe an attack or military strike made against an enemy's [or potential enemy's] weapons, communications, transport, etc. before they can be used*)

Examples:
- A: *It's really down to you to **pre-empt** another fiasco at head office.*

  B: *Why me? Any suggestions I make are made a mockery of.*
- *The Government should have **pre-empted** the unrest that was brought about by its policy of allowing unlimited immigration into the country.*
- *Officially, Israel's **pre-emptive** strike against Iraq's nuclear installations did not comply with international regulations, but, off the record, most governments were grateful that a clear future threat had been nipped in the bud.*

Makeshift (Temporary, imperfect--*often used for accommodation*)

Examples:
- *They all took the mickey out of a **makeshift** tree-house I built in the garden for my son. I'm not an adept carpenter by any stretch of the imagination.*
- *The refugees are going through a great deal of hardship in having to live in the **makeshift** shelter organised by the United Nations troops. Medicines and food supplies are dwindling too.*

To build up, build-up (noun)

i.   (To increase, accumulation--*especially over a period of time*)
Examples:

- *A massive backlog of claims has **built up** over the Christmas period.*
- *I don't want to **build up** your hopes too high, but the odds are you'll be shortlisted for the prize.*
- *The Government have pledged to reduce the **build-up** of patients waiting to have operations. New regulations, however, will take some time to be phased in.*

ii. (To make someone/something seem important)
Examples:
- In the aftermath of the war, the press **built him up** to be a hero, but in reality he bluffed his way to the top of the army and was a fairly pathetic leader of men.
- The whole issue was **built up** to such a degree that most people had lost track of its original purpose.

iii. (To regain weight--*usually after suffering from an illness*)
Example:
- Your sister was asking after you yesterday, and I told her that you needed **building up** before you could face the world again.

To huddle, huddled (To keep close together, often for warmth or because of fear, [huddled] kept close together)

Examples:
- As the cold nights drew in, the Jones family often found themselves **huddling** around the fire.
- The only stumbling block remaining was what the troops would do with the many refugees they had found **huddled** together under makeshift tents.

Cue (A signal for action, something said or done by an actor that tells another actor that it is his turn to speak or do something--*note the expression "**on cue**", which means on time. It is used to express the idea of something happening when one thought it might.*)

Examples:
- Writing off his wife's car was the final straw: that was his **cue** to stop driving.
- When she started to disrupt the party, that was our **cue** to leave. The horrible "music" was doing my head in anyway.
- One actor to another:
When I stick out my leg, that's your **cue** to waffle on about your illness.
- The outlook seemed quite promising until I noticed some dark clouds overhead…and then, right **on cue**, it started pouring with rain . I can't get my head round English weather at all.

To cram

i. (To study intensively for an exam, usually at the last minute)
Examples:
- You'll have to put it tactfully to Mrs. Smith, but unless her son **crams** for this exam, he doesn't stand a chance of getting through. He's left it a bit late.
- There's always a frenzy of activity just before exams. Our students tend to **cram**, many of them doing nothing during the rest of the year…but those ones get their comeuppance.

ii. (To pack things or people into a small space)
Examples:

- Sorry to butt in, but there are more than twenty fans **crammed** into the entrance hall, waiting to see you.
- I felt a bit uneasy having to **cram** £2,000 into my top pocket. I didn't relish the idea of travelling on the underground like that.

To be under no illusions (To know and understand what is really happening instead of imagining how things could be, to be realistic)

Examples:
- Don't worry, I'm **under no illusions**: I know that meeting my mother will bring out the worst in him. I'm dreading it.
- Let me make it clear: we're acting **under no illusions**. We are quite aware that, by and large, our competitors have cornered the market.

Yob (Hooligan, an uncultured, uneducated, violent youth)

Examples:

- We shouldn't be complacent about the recent reduction in crime. We still have many pubs crammed full of drunken **yobs** who get a buzz out of causing havoc in town centres on their way home.
- He's quite streetwise; he knows how to stick up for himself if he comes across any **yobs** on his way home.

To be off one's head/rocker, to be out of one's mind (To be crazy or mad) **Colloquial**

Examples:
- You must have been **off your head** trying to rub her up the wrong way. You know what a temper she has. She could have killed you.
- He'll be in his element spending time with John. He's also **off his rocker.** They will really take to each other.
- He left her stranded at the side of the road with no means of getting home. He must be totally **out of his mind**.

To grovel (To flatter, be excessively pleasant to someone, often because one feels guilty about previous bad behaviour, or because one wants something from them)

Examples:
- I'm under no illusions: I know they will want me to **grovel** before they let me back into the club. No way!
- Let him wallow in his misery before forcing him to make a **grovelling** apology.

*"He's quite streetwise; he knows how to stick up for himself if he comes across any **yobs** on his way home."*

(see page 73)

NEWS REPORT FROM KOSOVO

REPORTER: *I'm standing at the border of Serbia and Kosovo, where there has been an upsurge in violence over the last few days. In the aftermath of the Serbian invasion, the Kosovan Albanians have had to survive in makeshift huts. Some of the elder members of the community have been huddled around campfires. It is a pathetic sight.*

The resistance from the Kosovan soldiers is dwindling and the ones that remain feel jaded. Off the record, NATO commanders have given a pledge that, if called upon, they will make pre-emptive strikes on Serbian forces, so that they are unable to carry out new, frenzied attacks. The UN are also building up forces along the border to help feed the homeless, but both sides are making a mockery of the aid program.

The public back home should be under no illusions: neither side is going to back down without a fight, and it's going to be ordinary citizens who are left to wallow in perpetual misery.

CONVERSATION BETWEEN TWO MOTHERS

HELEN: *You know, bringing up two boisterous kids is doing my head in.*

ALISON: *I know what you mean. My sister, who I must admit is quite adept at coping with her three children, has decided to have a fourth.*

HELEN: *She must be off her head!*

ALISON: *Yes, especially as her eldest boy has turned out to be a yob.*

HELEN: *Well, I suppose some people get a buzz out of living a hectic, stressful life.*

ALISON: *Her husband does a little bit to help her in the house, but it's down to her to get the kids dressed and off to school.*

HELEN: *Well, at least she gets **some** help. I have to grovel just to get my husband to clear the table.*

ALISON: *I'm sure if there was a competition for mother of the year, my sister would be shortlisted.*

HELEN: *Good for her… I'd come last!*

CHOOSE THE CORRECT WORD FROM THOSE IN RED
Answers on page 135.

1. *These days there are so many drunken ᵃ(pledges/yobs/fiascos/bluffs) in England who seem to ᵇ(pre-empt/bluff their way through/get a buzz out of/wallow in) making unprovoked ᶜ(frenzied/grovelling/upsurging/perpetual) attacks on innocent victims walking home at night.*

2. *You should be ᵃ(off your head/under no illusions/dwindling/shortlisted): this is a very tricky exam indeed and one which you will not be able to pass simply by ᵇ(pre-empting/phasing in/getting a buzz out of/bluffing your way through)it.*

3. *The Ministry of Defence cannot make a ᵃ(fiasco/pledge/upsurge/huddle) to the army that they will reverse ᵇ(dwindling/shortlisted/grovelling/makeshift) stocks of weapons to fight the war. It will be ᶜ(on cue for/phased out by/down to/made a mockery of) each individual army division to make the best of what they have.*

4. *Two of the "novelists" who made the ᵃ(upsurge/huddle/makeshift/shortlist) for the Oxford Prize In Literature were sportsmen who have never read a book in their lives. What a ᵇ(fiasco/bluff/aftermath/back-down)!*

5. *I've been revising all day trying to ᵃ(wallow in/huddle/cram/pre-empt) for these exams. It's ᵇ(down to me/fiasco/jaded/doing my head in).*

6. *The manager has become very ᵃ(perpetual/adept/jaded/boisterous) at ᵇ(grovelling/ wallowing/making a mockery of/building) his players up into something they're not. Their performance last Saturday was quite ᶜ(pathetic/adept/makeshift/built up).*

7. *In this atmosphere of ᵃ(pathetic/grovelling/perpetual/boisterous) mistrust, it has become impossible to ᵇ(pre-empt/wallow in/get a buzz out of/phase in) what is likely to happen next.*

8. *It's entirely your own fault, and I won't forgive you. So don't come ᵃ(huddling/grovelling/ cramming/wallowing) to me. You'll have to ᵇ(grovel/bluff/dwindle/wallow) in your own regret for a while…but your dinner's on the table.*

9. *After the Government ᵃ(phased in/backed down/built up/called their bluff) on introducing stricter visa requirements for foreigners wishing to enter the country, there was an immediate ᵇ(huddle/cram/shortlist/upsurge) in applications.*

10. *In the ᵃ(aftermath/fiasco/frenzy/build-up) of the earthquake, the villagers had no choice but to live in ᵇ(boisterous/dwindling/makeshift/shortlisted) accommodation, and as there was no heating available, they had to ᶜ(wallow in/huddle together/pledge themselves/make a mockery of themselves) for warmth.*

11. *Last Friday night he was behaving in his usual crazy ᵃ(perpetual/jaded/makeshift/boisterous) manner. And then, right ᵇ(on pledge/on cue/adept/in the aftermath), he walked into the kitchen table and smashed a glass onto the floor. He then tried to pick up the pieces of glass with his teeth. My thoughts about him were right the first time I met him: he's completely ᶜ(pathetic/jaded/yobbish/off his rocker).*

12. *The Members of Parliament had been sitting in the House of Commons for over ten hours debating the proposed new tax laws. They all looked fed up and ᵃ(jaded/adept/pathetic/ huddled). These laws, if they were ever come into effect, would have to be ᵇ(pre-empted/ phased in/buzzed out/built up) over a period of five years, by which time they would be out of date. This really ᶜ(wallows in/gets a buzz out of/crams/makes a mockery of) our democratic process.*

Lesson One

To take someone through something (To describe a situation, to explain something to someone)

Examples:

- Policeman:
  Take me through exactly what was going on in your mind when you inadvertently passed a red light… madam.
- Commentator to footballer:
  Can you take us through your second goal? The goalkeeper looked absolutely gobsmacked.

To shift

i. (To move/budge, to change one's direction--note the noun "**shift**", which means a change of position or belief, see 4th example below--*also note the adjective "shifty", which is used to describe a person who looks like he should not be trusted.)*

Examples:

- *The date of the meeting has **shifted** to Tuesday. It's down to you to tell the others.*
- *Trying to find a way of **shifting** this sofa is doing my head in.*
- *The new Government are playing down the fact that their objectives have **shifted** since taking office. The voters were wrong to build up their hopes that things were going to change.*
- *Take my word for it: there has definitely been a **shift** in attitudes since he became managing director.*
- *I was lulled into a false sense of security until I noticed his **shifty** eyes.*

ii. (To remove a stain, to get rid of a minor illness)

Examples:

- *This detergent will stand you in good stead for the future. It **shifts** stains without a fuss.*
- *Patient to Doctor:*
  *This cold doesn't seem to be **shifting**. Can you prescribe something else to help me shrug it off ?*

Skirmish (A small fight/minor battle)

Examples:
- The rebels refused to back down over their demands for the Russian army to release some of its prisoners. This resulted in countless **skirmishes** all over the capital.
- It was a foregone conclusion that there would be a few **skirmishes** between the parties during the run-up to the election.

To unnerve/unnerving (To scare, to make one feel nervous, frightening/worrying)

Examples:
- He tried to **unnerve** me by building his brother up to be a real tough guy. But I knew all along that he was just a wimp.
- I must say, I find the upsurge in yobbish behaviour in modern society to be rather **unnerving**. The Government's recent attempts to improve behaviour in schools are only skimming the surface.

Hype (Intensive promotion)

Examples:
- The **hype** surrounding her latest CD was a bit over the top; it's really nothing to write home about.
- All the **hype** going around about his new book put me off buying it. I'm very choosy about what I read these days.

To string someone along (To mislead or deceive someone by making them believe one thinks the same way, or has the same desires--note the phrase "**to string a sentence together**", which means to be able to express oneself clearly. It is generally used in a negative sense to indicate that someone isn't very intelligent)

Examples:
- She felt jaded by the whole affair and didn't cotton on to the fact that he was just **stringing her along** until the end.
- Don't take her word for it; I reckon she's simply **stringing you along**. You do need to get to the bottom of this.
- Some of these yobs can't even **string a sentence together.** 'Thick' is an understatement to describe these people.

Pushover Colloquial

i. (Someone with whom it is easy to get one's own way--*see Practical Everyday English, page 165, easy to convince*)
Examples:
- *She may be down to earth, but by no stretch of the imagination is she a **pushover**. You'll have to come up with something much more convincing.*
- *He's sulking because he thought his mum would be a **pushover** when it came to lending him her car. He turned out to be very mistaken.*

ii. (Easy to get/pass/beat)
Examples:
- A: *I'm going to stick my neck out and say I bet the exam is going to be a real **pushover** this year.*
- B: *But you still won't get through it.*
- *You should weigh up the other team very carefully before writing them off as **pushovers***

To be endowed with (To be born/blessed with, to possess--*note the noun "**endowment**", which is a formal donation of money made to an organisation or charity*)

Examples:
- *Even though he can be quite boisterous at times, he has been **endowed with** a wonderfully good nature.*
- *She is quite adept at bluffing her way through a seminar, but that's because she is **endowed with** her mother's brains.*
- *I wouldn't put it past him to try and stop the generous **endowment** his wife has made to the college.*

Uproar (Angry protest or criticism)

Examples:
- *There was **uproar** from jazz fans when, despite all the hype, Jazz FM started to play bland, hotel lounge music.*
- *By and large, the public didn't create much **uproar** when the electoral system was changed. Few people these days bother to take any interest in anything which requires them to think.*

To undermine (To ridicule someone/something, to make someone in a position of authority feel worthless/weak)

Examples:
- Confidence in our sporting ability in this country has been **undermined** by the fact that in recent years we have become the laughing stock of the world.
- They didn't want to come over as if they were **undermining** his authority, although it's quite apparent to anyone following this story that power has shifted away from him.
- I'm under no illusions: you've been **undermining** me all these years and a grovelling apology won't make any difference now.

Policeman: "**Take me through** exactly what was going on in your mind when you inadvertently passed a red light... madam."

(see page 78)

Chapter Six
Lesson Two

To dumb down, dumbing down (To make something which should be difficult or intellectually demanding easy or undemanding, so that it is more accessible to the general public, making something too easy--*a negative term*)

Examples:
- *I don't like to undermine teachers, but even they will admit, off the record, that the subjects they're teaching our teenagers, have been dramatically **dumbed down** since we were at school.*
- *It is quite pathetic to see how many of the quality newspapers are guilty of **dumbing down** just to increase sales…but my wife thinks I'm being pompous.*
- *The upsurge in university applications is probably down to the perpetual **dumbing down** of entrance exams. Even my thick brother can get in!*

To emerge, emerging (To present oneself, often after being hidden or unknown, to become evident, [emerging] up and coming--*see earlier, page 11*)

Examples:
- *He **emerged** from the corner of the room, which had been crammed full of tourists. He must have nearly passed out in that heat.*
- *It soon **emerged** that the police had tried to pre-empt another frenzied attack by the demonstrators.*
- *In the aftermath of the slump, some of the **emerging** industrial nations had been building up their defence forces.*

Disgruntled (Angry and dissatisfied because things have not turned out as expected)

Examples:
- *It is clear that many members of the public are **disgruntled** because they feel the Government have been stringing them along. But I'm never taken in by any of the hype politicians come out with.*
- *The shareholders are **disgruntled** at the fact that some of the directors have been raking it in this year. The directors claim, on the other hand, that as they have invested their own personal wealth in the company, they are entitled to reap the rewards.*

To grate on someone
(To irritate or annoy someone--*usually through a noise, habit or type of behaviour--also note the adjective "**grating**", which generally describes an unpleasant sound which is difficult to tolerate*)

Examples:
- The dumbing down of BBC news will definitely **grate on you** after a while. They talk to us like children. So patronising!
- A: Her loud laughter is beginning to **grate on me**.
- B: Yes, it's doing my head in as well.
- It was the sound of her **grating** voice that was my cue to get going. I know it wasn't very tactful of me but I couldn't wait to get home.

Blatant
(Obvious, clear, indiscreet, unashamed--*often used for something negative*)

Examples:
- His perpetual **blatant** lies have led everyone to mistrust him. He and his honest brother are like chalk and cheese.
- Grovelling is often said to be a **blatant** expression of fear.
- Telling him he was an absolute pushover was being a bit **blatant**. You could have gone about it in a more subtle way.

To die down
(To become calmer/quieter--*used for a situation*)

Examples:
- Once the current uproar has **died down**, we hope the other row over who has the right to receive the endowment will blow over.
- After the storm had **died down**, we all tried cramming into the car. It was a bit of a fiasco.

To keep at bay
(To prevent something/someone harmful from happening/approaching)

Examples:
- Once the flu symptoms have died down, you'll need to take vitamin C to **keep** a further virus **at bay** and help build up your defence system again.
- You'll have to comply with the new regulations if you want to **keep** the taxman **at bay**. I'll take you through the correct procedure if you like.

To brand (To label someone, to cause someone to be known as a particular type of person--*used in a negative sense*)

Examples:
- It has emerged that many people **branded** him a liar even before his authority began to be undermined.
- Most people wanted to give him the benefit of the doubt until, amid all this scandal, he was **branded** a womaniser.

Grounding (Training, education, instruction--*note the word "grounding" is often accompanied by the adjective "good"*)

Examples:
- After the new laws have been phased in, we will all need a good **grounding** in European legal administration.
- All of the candidates shortlisted for the job have a good **grounding** in economics. They are lucky enough to have escaped our dumbed-down education system.

To unveil (To show something for the first time, to reveal)

Examples:
- The Mayor **unveiled** a new statue of Queen Victoria before waffling on about overseas trade. Pompous fool!
- There was an uneasy silence as the marketing director **unveiled** his plans for the coming year. He said he was aiming to corner the market in home furnishings. We all have our doubts, and fear he's clutching at straws.

"A: Her loud laughter is beginning to **grate on me**.
B: Yes, it's doing my head in as well."

(see page 83)

Lesson Three

A bitter pill to swallow (Something that is hard to accept, but must be accepted)

Examples:
- What emerged from the discussion was that the project had been a complete flop, and will be a **bitter pill** for everyone **to swallow**.
- As soon as Maria first set eyes on her newborn baby boy, she knew that he wasn't going to be endowed with the good looks of his elder brother. This was a very **bitter pill** for her **to swallow**.

Not on (not acceptable behaviour) **Colloquial**

Examples:
- We won't stand for such blatant racism in this company. **It's just not on**!
- Telling her she had a grating laugh **was not really on**, and you shouldn't have taken the mickey out of her silly voice either.

(See picture below)

To alienate

    i.   (To make someone feel unsympathetic/hostile towards one's views or actions)
         Examples:
- As time goes by, the Government are increasingly **alienating** the voters.
- In trying to keep creditors at bay, the directors have **alienated** the shareholders.

    ii.   (To become separated from--*generally used in an emotional sense*)
         Examples:
- He could never appreciate the hardships which his parents went through in bringing him up, and became **alienated** from them in later life.
- I know it sounds like a cliché, but many people believe that the leaders of the party have become **alienated** from the ordinary members.

Slapdash (Careless, hurried, done without thinking or planning)

         Examples:
- '**Slapdash**' is the adjective I'd use to describe the proposed new layout of the entrance hall. The owners are going to be a bit disgruntled when they see it.
- He's quite good at shrugging off criticism, so he won't be too touchy if you tell him this time he has been rather **slapdash** in the way he approached the project.

To make a comeback

    i.   (To be successful again after a long break--*often used for a musician, sports person or politician*)
         Examples:
- It was a foregone conclusion that he wouldn't be able to **make a comeback**. Everyone knows he's well past it.
- When he saw how well his old friend Steve was playing golf, it was his cue to try to **make a comeback**. He didn't know what he was letting himself in for.

    ii.   (To be fashionable again)
         Examples:
- It was thought that the Fiat Uno, once the best selling car of its kind, might **make a comeback** this year, but sales have continued to dwindle.

- *The mini-skirt got a lot of hype when it came out in the sixties, and now many people are happy to see that it's **making a comeback**…especially my husband!*

Slim   (Not very likely--*generally used with "chances" or "odds"–note the most common meaning of "slim", which readers will presumably already know, is the opposite of "fat". Unlike "thin", "slim" is a positive word to describe someone. See 3rd example below*)

Examples:
- *Having alienated the general public to such a degree, the <u>chances</u> of the Government being re-elected are very **slim**.*
- Parent: *What are the <u>odds</u> on my son Nick being shortlisted for a place at Oxford?*
  Teacher: *Very **slim**, I'm afraid.*
  Parent: *That's a bitter pill for us to have to swallow.*
- *Since she was branded "fat" by the press, she has become determined to be **slim** again…then she'll be ready to make a comeback.*

To pester   (To annoy someone by continually asking or telling them to do something, to nag--*see Practical Everyday English, page 61–note that a person who is perpetually pestering people can be called a "**pest**"*)

Examples:
- *When he started to **pester** me for more attention, the impatient side of my nature emerged.*
- *Sorry to **pester** you, but could you take me through the new data system again? I lost track of what you were saying.*
- *I'm feeling rather jaded tonight, so don't be a **pest**!*

To amend   (To change, alter or correct a document, a text or law--*note the expression "**to make amends for**", which means to compensate for a mistake*)

Examples:
- *They will be phasing in a new law to deal with sex offenders, once it has been **amended** by Parliament.*
- A: *You'll have to **amend** the book yourself if you think it needs dumbing down.*
  B: *That's not what I'm saying. Don't be so touchy. I just think you've been a bit slapdash, that's all.*
- *You don't have to grovel if you wish to **make amends for** what you've done. 'Sorry' will be sufficient.*

To go/buy for a song (To be sold/buy very cheaply)

Examples:
- When one weighs up all the failings of the business, it's not surprising it **went for a song**.
- We **bought** the house **for a song** thirty years ago, when we could hardly make ends meet. Now it's worth a fortune and my jealous friends are feeling disgruntled.

To stray (To move away from the subject, to wander from the main path--*note that a "stray"dog or cat is one that has permanently lost its owner or never had one*)

Examples:
- The course gave me a good grounding in basic French, but my mind did begin to **stray** towards the end. Maybe I'm past it and should give up on the idea of studying anything.
- The driver was slightly unnerved by the fact that a few sheep had **strayed** on to the road.
- He alienates the neighbours by feeding **stray** cats in his garden. They huddle together outside his house and make real pests of themselves.

INTERVIEWER: *Many of the voters who fell for your pre-election* hype *are now beginning to feel* disgruntled, *saying that you have been coming out with* blatant *lies. Have your objectives* shifted?

PRIME MINISTER: *No, not at all. Let me* take you through *what had been going on over the last ten years, before we took over. The previous government ran down all the public services, which* alienated *the entire British public. They were also guilty of* stringing *the people* along *on many other issues. Now the excitement of having a new government is* dying down, *so we have to sort out the mess we were left in. It has* emerged *that things are going to take longer than expected, and this is a* bitter pill to swallow *for some people, but we will be* unveiling *new strategies in the coming weeks.*

INTERVIEWER: *As far as education is concerned, you have been accused of* dumbing down *the syllabuses and* undermining *the teachers' authority.*

PRIME MINISTER: *Well, for many years schools have been under-achieving. You know,* it's just not on. *We expect all our children to have a good basic* grounding *in the main subjects, but many of our youngsters are* straying *from the right path when they leave school. I don't want to be* branded *as a teacher-hater but I would like it to be known that things have to change.*

Hey Martin!

Where were you on Friday night? We all went for a drink at the Coach and Horses. Your friend Tim, who is not endowed with *brains even when he's sober, and* grates on *me more and more each time I see him, got involved in a* skirmish *with another guy who he said was* pestering *his girlfriend. Tim thought this bloke was going to be a* pushover, *as he was half his size, but the little guy was not* unnerved *by the prospect of a fight, even though his chances of success were* slim. *Anyway, as they got stuck in, there was* uproar *in the pub, and I tried to* keep *the two of them* at bay. In the end, they shook hands and bought each other drinks. It's funny how things turn out!*

Hope we can get together next week and catch up.
All the best
John

Chapter Six: **Exercise**

CHOOSE THE CORRECT WORD FROM THOSE IN RED
Answers on page 134

1. *We're going to have to lay off more staff than I thought. It is indeed a* ᵃ*(blatant lie/bitter pill to swallow/hype/uproar). So I've asked Jenny, our employment lawyer, to come to a meeting and* ᵇ*(make a comeback/unveil/brand/take us through) the correct procedure.*

2. *I do not believe all the* ᵃ*(hype/uproar/shifting/alienation) coming from the Government ministers that our public exams are going to become rigorous and more difficult to pass. Most children these days lack a good* ᵇ*(pushover/grounding/branding/hype) in mathematics and English, and have become unfortunate victims of our* ᶜ*(slim/amended/dumbed-down/undermined) education system.*

3. *I don't want to* ᵃ*(unveil/shift/brand/undermine) my husband's authority in front of the children, and I certainly wouldn't like to* ᵇ*(alienate him/string him along/amend him/disgruntle him) at these times when I know he needs my support, but I do often wonder whether he is* ᶜ*(unveiled with/endowed with/emerged with/amended with) a brain.*

4. *There's no point in trying to* ᵃ*(pester me/grate on me/string me/shift me) along with your* ᵇ*(disgruntled/blatant/unnerving/grounding) lies. I know exactly what you are up to and it's just* ᶜ*(not on/a pushover/an uproar/slapdash).*

5. *Daniel says that your presence at parents' meetings with teachers* ᵃ*(brands/shifts/unnerves/pesters) him. He would much rather you express your thoughts in a letter to the school if you feel* ᵇ*(blatant/in uproar/pushed over/disgruntled) about something.*

6. *Jane is clearly a very bright girl, but she needs to spend much more time on preparing her written work; it's far too* ᵃ*(slapdash/dumbed-down/amended/slim). Also, she very often* ᵇ*(shifts/strays/undermines/pesters) from the subject.*

7. *What has* ᵃ*(emerged/shifted/amended/unveiled) from these discussions is that if we do sell the business, we cannot afford to let it* ᵇ*(be endowed/make a comeback/go for a song/die down). Remember, we have creditors to* ᶜ*(pester/amend/endow/keep at bay).*

8. *It wasn't so long ago when the music media* ᵃ*(endowed/branded/shifted/pestered) him as passé. But now he seems to be making something of a* ᵇ*(uproar/comeback/pushover/skirmish) and his chances of regaining his former popularity are not as* ᶜ*(slim/branded/disgruntled/shifted) as they once were.*

9. *Economists keep warning us that there will be a* ᵃ*(undermining/skirmish/shift/grounding) of financial power from west to east and that the U.S in particular needs to* ᵇ*(unveil/endow/hype/amend) new strategies to take account of this phenomenon.*

10. *She knows that her father is a complete* ᵃ*(uproar/stray/blatant/pushover) and that she doesn't need to* ᵇ*(shift/pester/string along/alienate) him for too long before she gets her own way. Men! They're all the same. Their behaviour and annoying habits* ᶜ*(grate/disgruntle/ die down/unveil) on all of us suffering women*

11. *In order to avoid unpleasant* ᵃ*(dumbing-down/skirmishes/hypes/pushovers)in this fragile political coalition we have recently formed, we will,unfortunately, need to* ᵇ*(unnerve/stray/ amend/unveil) our policies.*

12. *At first there was* ᵃ*(hype/branding/skirmish/uproar) amongst public sector workers when the Government announced a cutback in local council jobs, but now that the anger has* ᵇ*(died down/gone for a song/shifted/amended), most people have reluctantly accepted reality.*

Lesson One

Paralytic (Very drunk--*note these other slang words for drunk: "wasted", "wrecked", "smashed", "hammered", "plastered". There are many more, too numerous to be listed here*) **Slang**

Examples:
- When I was young, I didn't go around getting **paralytic** every Friday night. I don't want to pester you, but deep down, there must be something going on.
- I think she's keeping a low profile after she got **paralytic** at the summer office party. You would cringe if you saw the wimp she tried to kiss.

To curb (To control/restrain)

Examples:

- When the excitement of Christmas dies down, people usually **curb** their spending…apart from my wife!
- One thing has emerged from my visit to the doctor: I will have to **curb** my appetite. He was quite blatant with me.

To beggar belief/description (To be too extraordinary to be believed or described)

Examples:
- A: How could your father, of all people, take the mickey out of me for being prudish?

  B: I know. It does **beggar belief**, doesn't it?
- The sight of him grovelling to the boss **beggars description**. You should have been there. Most enlightening!

To sap (To weaken/take away one's strength, energy or confidence--*often used with "of"*)

Examples:
- As the years go by, I find my job **sapping** more and more of my strength. I'm not sure for how long I can put up with it.
- You should bear in mind that after a weekend of hill walking, you will feel jaded and **sapped** _of_ energy.

- An hour of listening to my boss have a go at me for everything I'd done wrong last week **sapped** me _of_ my confidence. I feel like handing in my notice.

To head off

i.   (To leave/get off--see *Practical Everyday English, page 121, meaning iv*)
Examples:
- I must be **heading off**; I've got to go round to Peter's this evening. I hope he's not paralytic by the time I get there.
- We **headed off** around 6am. The journey up the mountain road was a bit unnerving.

ii.   (To prevent an attack or other disturbance)
Examples:
- The police were a bit slapdash in trying to **head off** unrest amongst the protesters. They needlessly alienated everyone.
- Due to the Government's complacency, the Prime Minister, who had also been lulled into a false sense of security, ended up trying to **head off** a revolt by members of his own party.

To give someone a taste of their own medicine (To do to someone what they often do to others--*a negative expression, but not always very serious*)

Examples:
- She usually gets a kick out of being nasty to people. This time, I've **given her a taste of her own medicine**.
- He knows I'm squeamish because I nearly passed out when he showed me that horrible picture. It's time to **give him a taste of his own medicine**. He doesn't know what he has let himself in for.

Sceptical (Non-believing/Non-trusting)

Examples:
- I don't wish to dwell on the matter but I'm still very **sceptical** about whether he's the right person to get to the bottom of the problem.
- Why are you so **sceptical**? Can't you see that we are already beginning to reap the rewards?

To make a beeline for something/someone (To head for somewhere quickly because one really wants to go there, to hurry directly towards someone)

Examples:
- *Even though it was his uncle's funeral, immediately afterwards they **made a beeline for** the pub. It's not really on, is it?*
- A: *I suppose it was a bit blatant, but I **made a beeline for** her as soon as she entered the club.*

  B: *She must be off her head if she fancies you.*

Turmoil (Chaos, disorder or confusion)

Examples:
- *The National Health Service, the newspapers keep telling us, is in perpetual **turmoil**. Journalists often just jump on the bandwagon and go way over the top in their criticism of this marvellous institution.*
- *It's quite apparent that his life is in **turmoil**. This scandal will not just blow over.*

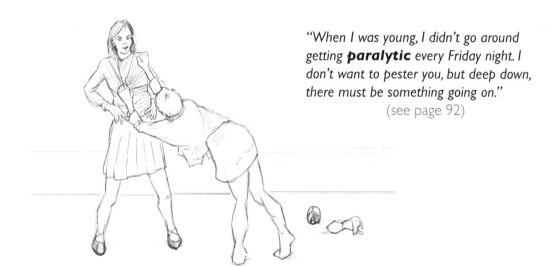

*"When I was young, I didn't go around getting **paralytic** every Friday night. I don't want to pester you, but deep down, there must be something going on."*
(see page 92)

To envisage (To foresee/imagine something is likely to happen)

Examples:
- *He doesn't even have a basic grounding in economics. I don't **envisage** his position as Chancellor of the Exchequer being a permanent one.*
- *Nobody **envisaged** him making such a comeback at his age. Many of his rivals are gobsmacked by his success.*

Lesson Two

To whinge (To complain in an annoying way)

Examples:
- She's likes to **whinge** about what a handful her son is, but the truth of the matter is that she gets flustered far too easily.
- I think if we nip the thing in the bud now, it will stop him **whingeing** later on. You know what a pest he can be.

Bolshy (Confrontational, rebellious, always answers back when told off or ordered to do something) **Colloquial**

Examples:
- The staff are unlikely to comply with the new regulations. They're a **bolshy** lot and it's hard to get them to budge.
- It's true, she was very **bolshy** with him, but I think it was warranted; he's such a whinger.

A sucker/glutton for punishment (A masochist, someone who appears to enjoy struggling in life or getting into trouble--*generally used in a humorous, non-serious way*)

Examples:
- I keep losing to him at tennis, but every week I build up my hopes and convince myself that the following week will turn out differently. It never does. I must be a sucker for **punishment**.
- He was branded a **glutton for punishment** after he decided to go to court for the third time. Nobody seems to be able to get through to him that he needs to curb his passion for litigation.

To deprive of, deprived (To take away someone's pleasures, rights or power, disadvantaged)

Examples:
- 'Disgruntled' is an understatement as to how parents will feel if the new government **deprives them** of child benefit.
- Life is a hardship for many **deprived** children who are not endowed with wealthy parents.

To be spoken for (To have a permanent partner in life, to be married, to be promised to someone else--*note that 'already' is often used with this expression*)

Examples:
- A: *It's not on to make a beeline for somebody who is already **spoken for**. Surely, he wouldn't do that?*
  B: *I wouldn't put it past him!*
- *I'm sorry if you feel we've been stringing you along, but we did clearly point out that the car was already **spoken for**.*

To flourish (To do well, to exist successfully)

Examples:
- *I'm a bit sceptical as to how a business with such a low profile can **flourish** in the modern-day economic climate.*
- *I don't want to jump on the bandwagon, but football will never **flourish** in the United States until everyone gets a good grounding in the basics of the game.*

Rift (A division and break in friendly relations between people--*often caused by a disagreement*)

Examples:
- *The **rift** between them will not be repaired until their anger has died down. Someone has to get to the bottom of what's going on.*
- *The current **rift** in the Labour Party has undermined the Prime Minister's authority. I've lost track of how many of his so-called friends have spoken out against him.*

To dabble (To take part in a certain type of business or activity only from time to time)

Examples:
- *He used only to **dabble** in stocks and shares, but when he saw how his friends were raking it in, he took it up full time.*
- *He has always wanted to **dabble** in politics and he won't be happy until he gets it out of his system. His wife, on the other hand, is absolutely dreading it.*

A dark horse
(A person whom no one really knows, but who later reveals himself to be different and more interesting than first thought or a person who exceeds expectations in a competition or election)

Examples:
- *He comes over as a wimp, with no opinions, but take my word for it: once you draw him out of his shell, you'll see he's quite **a dark horse***
- *John thinks Jim Taylor could prove to be **a dark horse** and win Wimbledon this year. I'm rather sceptical and don't envisage any surprises.*

To embark on
(To begin something which could take a long time to complete)

Examples:
- *I sometimes wonder why I **embarked on** such a course of action. I managed to alienate everyone.*
- *The Opposition have **embarked on** a policy of disruption during parliamentary debates on the proposed new tax laws. They claim there are still many loopholes unclosed which will make a mockery of the justice system, but these politicians are simply clutching at straws, fully aware that their minority leaves then powerless.*

*"I don't want to jump on the bandwagon, but football will never **flourish** in the United States until everyone gets a good grounding in the basics of the game."*

(see page 96)

Lesson Three

To bow to pressure or someone's wishes (To change one's actions, plans, or direction because of outside pressure)

Examples:
- We're not going to **bow to** such blatant pressure from a few disgruntled shareholders.
- I'm under no illusions: I know I'll have to **bow to** her wishes eventually. Women always get their own way in the end.

To scrape the barrel (To struggle to find a good solution, an answer, or the right person of quality)

Examples:
- The police are playing down the fact that they are having to **scrape the barrel** as far as obtaining any fresh evidence is concerned. They haven't really got much to go on.
- It would be quite enlightening to see their selection procedure. They must be **scraping the barrel** if they feel they need to take a fool like that on.

Over one's head (Too complex, beyond someone's comprehension--*often used with "to go" where a remark, comment or joke which has not registered with or been understood by someone is the subject of the sentence. It is often used with "straight"*)

Examples:
- I'm sorry, but this is way **over my head**. Could I ask you to dumb it down a little so that even a thicko like me can understand it?
- She made some witty reference to the fact that he had become the laughing stock of the village, but it **went** straight **over his head**.

To turn over a new leaf (To change one's character or behaviour for the better)

Examples:
- I don't want to sound sceptical, but I can't envisage him **turning over a new leaf**; he's getting on for seventy.
- I think it's time you t**urned over a new leaf** and stuck up for yourself. Give him a taste of his own medicine and get your own back.

"If you think...you've got another think coming" ("If you think...you can think again...you're wrong!") **Colloquial**

Examples:
- ***If you think*** *you can take the mickey out of me like that,* ***you've got another think coming****.*
- A: ***If he thinks*** *he's going to be shortlisted for promotion,* ***he's got another think coming****. Why don't you tell him?*
- B: *I wouldn't want to deprive you of that pleasure.*

To rub it in (To make someone's emotional suffering worse by reminding them of something unpleasant)

Examples:
- *He keeps reminding her that she's no longer slim, and seems to get a kick out of* ***rubbing it in****. Can't he see how distraught she is?*
- A: *Is it true you got plastered on your wedding night?*
- B: *O.K.! There's no need* ***to rub it in****.*

To bang one's head against a brick wall (To get nowhere, to feel that you are being ignored/not being listened to--*note this expression is often preceded by "like"*)

Examples:
- *Trying to get through to my husband that he must raise his fees if he wants to keep the creditors at bay is like* ***banging my head against a brick wall****.*
- *I've told them that they will have to amend the contract if they want to avoid turmoil later on, but I feel like I'm* ***banging my head against a brick wall****.*

To make a song and dance about something (To complain/ make a fuss about something--*see Practical Everyday English, page 3*)

Examples:
- *She* ***makes a song and dance about*** *bolshy Rita causing a rift in the office, but it goes over the boss's head.*
- *Listen, I'm not exactly flourishing in this job either, but that doesn't mean I have to go around* ***making a song and dance about*** *it.*

*"She made some witty reference to the fact that he had become the laughing stock of the village, but it went <u>straight</u> **over his head**"*
(see page 98)

To thrive (To succeed/do well/prosper, to live/survive on--*occasionally used to emphasise that ones loves [doing] something; i.e., not literally surviving, but greatly enjoying-see 3rd example below*)

Examples:
- *I nearly bowed to pressure from my parents not to marry Tom. They said I was scraping the barrel and could do better. I'm glad I didn't listen…because our marriage is **thriving**.*
- *He **thrives** <u>on</u> picking up antique furniture for a song, then pestering dealers to buy it the next day.*
- *I **thrive** <u>on</u> chocolate and cakes and always make a beeline for desserts at buffet lunches. It's a habit that I'm going to have to curb.*

To cash in on something (To take advantage of a situation, to exploit)

Examples:
- *There was uproar from Members of Parliament (MPs) who support the Government when the leader of the Opposition tried to **cash in on** the Prime Minister's recent unpopularity.*
- *Many ruthless businessmen are **cashing in on** the fact that the poor are not endowed with the means to escape poverty.*
- *If he thinks he is going to **cash in on** my misfortunes, he's got another think coming.*

Thank you for giving up your time today. I'm sorry to deprive you all of an evening with your families.

Up to the end of last year, the company's finances were in turmoil. Nobody envisaged this happening after we had embarked on a new policy of cashing in on the Government's decision to devalue the pound. At times, we were really scraping the barrel for new ideas and it was true that a rift had begun to appear between the directors of the company.

After bowing to much pressure, in January we decided to turn over a new leaf by curbing our unnecessary expenses. We needed to head off almost certain bankruptcy, as our creditors were whingeing about not being paid.

Now, I can happily say the company is flourishing again. Business is thriving ,especially in Europe, giving us a great opportunity to invest seriously, and not just dabble, in new and exciting products.

I'd like to thank each and every one of you for taking the time and effort to save this business.

JOHN: *You know, the amount that Peter drinks beggars belief.*

JAMES: *Why? Was he paralytic again on Sunday?*

JOHN: *What do you think?*

JAMES: *He is just a sucker for punishment. He doesn't know when to stop. Poor chap!*

JOHN: *On Sunday in the pub, he decided to make a beeline for this pretty Italian girl. I tried to tell him she was already spoken for, but it went straight over his head. It's like banging your head against a brick wall, trying to tell him how to behave.*

JAMES: *Yes, and I'll tell you something else: if you think you're inviting him to my 40th birthday party, you've got another think coming.*

JOHN: *Well, you brought that bolshy political activist Jim Smith to mine, so I'm thinking about giving you a taste of your own medicine. No, but seriously, you'll see, there's no need to make a song and dance about it; I'll make sure he's on his best behaviour.*

JAMES: *Oh really? I'm sorry but I'm very sceptical about that.*

JOHN: *OK, I have to get off here. See you tomorrow. Have a nice evening.*

Chapter Seven: **Exercise**

CHOOSE THE CORRECT WORD FROM THOSE IN RED
Answers on page 134

1. A: *Don't you think it's about time you* ^a*(embarked on/curbed/dabbled/headed off) your drinking habit? You've already lost your job because of it when you got* ^b*(paralytic flourished / sceptical/spoken for) last month.*
   B: *OK, OK. You don't have to* ^c*(scrape the barrel/go over my head/rub it in/bang your head against a brick wall).*

2. *On reflection, I'm not sure why we* ^a*(dabbled/embarked on/curbed/envisaged) this course of action. I'm now rather* ^b*(deprived/flourished/bolshy/sceptical) as to whether all the time and effort we've put in has been worth it.*

3. A: *I've got my eye on him. He's not what he seems you know; he's quite a* ^a*(dark horse/ whinger/bolshy/dabbler).*
   B: *Sorry to* ^b*(envisage you/sap you/deprive you/rub you in) of a new man, but he's well and truly* ^c*(curbed/spoken for/thriving/in turmoil). I saw him first!*

4. *If you think I'm going to let that* ^a*(dark horse/whinger/paralytic/bolshy) woman boss me around all day…*^b*(it will go over my head/you are scraping the barrel/you've got another think coming/I will turn over a new leaf). She* ^c*(thrives on/embarks on/deprives of/curbs) giving out orders.*

5. *My daughter is struggling in her French class, but I'm not going to* ^a*(scrape the barrel/make a song and dance about it/go over her head/turn over a new leaf). The last thing I want to do is* ^b*(sap/deprive/curb/thrive) her confidence. She's* ^c*(sapping/heading off/dabbling/ flourishing) in all her other subjects.*

6. *Somehow, I can't* ^a*(curb/envisage/embark/dabble) you living in the countryside. Before long, you'd be* ^b*(flourishing/thriving/whingeing/cashing in) about the boring night life.*

7. *How she could possibly think that he's the right man for the job* ^a*(goes over my head/ beggars belief/gives me a taste of my own medicine/heads me off). She's unaware of it, but she really is* ^b*(beggaring belief/turning over a new leaf/going over his head/scraping the barrel) employing that wimp. One day I'm going to put a useless person in her department just to* ^c*(give her a taste of her own medicine/scrape the barrel/deprive her/go over her head).*

8. *She* ^a*(dabbles/embarks/thrives/cashes) in witchcraft and black magic, which has caused a* ^b*(whinge/turmoil/rift/flourish) with her husband. He has pleaded with her to stop, but feels it's like* ^c*(turning over a new leaf/scraping the barrel/banging his head against a brick wall/ making a song and dance about it).*

9.   *When I'm at a buffet lunch I always* ᵃ*(turn over a new leaf/make a beeline/rub it in/cash in) for the sandwiches. Then I have to try everything else on offer, even if it makes me ill. I'm a real* ᵇ*(whinger/paralytic/dabbler/sucker for punishment).*

10.   *My husband has assured me that since the beginning of the year he has* ᵃ*(turned over a new leaf/bowed to pressure/given me a taste of my own medicine/made a beeline) and will now listen to me attentively. But deep down, I know all the instructions I give him will* ᵇ*(scrape the barrel/head off/beggar belief/go over his head).*

11.   *The President must devise a plan to* ᵃ*(bow to pressure/sap/head off/deprive) a citizens' revolution, otherwise the country will be plunged into* ᵇ*(rift/turmoil/deprivation/thriving).*

12.   *Many manufacturers in the UK have* ᵃ*(made a beeline/embarked on/rubbed it in/cashed in on) the devalued pound to increase sales of their goods abroad. This devaluation was brought about by the Government having* ᵇ*(beggared belief/bowed to pressure/flourished/scraped the barrel) from prominent businessmen.*

Chapter Eight
Lesson One

To mingle (to mix socially)

Examples:
- I think she finds it difficult to **mingle** with a boisterous crowd of guests.
- By and large, most people at the party **mingled**, and your cousin turned out to be quite a dark horse.

Trait (Characteristic)

Examples:
- He clearly has the **trait** of a winner in him; the rest of them will remain the laughing stock of world football.
- She has many of the **traits** of her grandmother, who was also very outgoing.

To lift a finger (To make an effort to help someone--*generally used in the negative*)

Examples:
- At the dinner all he did was take the mickey out of his mother-in-law. He **didn't lift a finger** to help his wife in the kitchen.
- A: While I've been doing the housework, you haven't **lifted a finger**.
  B: Oh, get off my back! I've got a lot on my plate at the moment.

To be overwhelmed, overwhelming (To be completely controlled by an emotional feeling, too much, over the top, greater than expected--*either positive or negative*)

Examples:
- He was **overwhelmed** with joy when they told him they were going to publish his book; now he will be able to reap the rewards of years of hard work.
- I do find him a bit **overwhelming** at times; he tends to take over any conversation I start and perpetually refers back to events in his own life..

- *Take my word for it: the response to your advertising campaign will be **overwhelming**.*

Plight (The difficult/dangerous/depressing situation)

Examples:
- *To say that the **plight** of these refugees is an unfortunate one is something of an understatement.*
- *We should be under no illusions that the **plight** of the Bengal tiger is going to improve.*

To be out of one's depth (To feel that one has insufficient knowledge or experience, to be with people who are more knowledgeable/better educated, or who perform at a much higher level)

Examples:
- *I felt a little out of **my depth** when he began to touch on scientific theories.*
- *He was trying to mingle with a group of Oxford professors, but was quite clearly totally **out of his depth.***
- *It has become increasingly apparent to me that quite a few of our players are **out of their depth** in the Premier League. They were all pathetic last Saturday.*

*"He was trying to mingle with a group of Oxford professors, but was quite clearly totally **out of his depth**."*

Teething problems (Initial problems--*note that when a baby is "teething" it means that his first teeth are coming through*)

Examples:
- If we manage to get over these **teething problems**, we should break even this year.
- How can I put it? Let's just say that when we got this project underway, we had more than a few **teething problems** relating to the layout of the building, but now things are definitely looking up.

To bring on (To cause--*often used in connection with illness*)

Examples:
- Whenever I talk to a doctor about my illness, I feel like I'm banging my head against a brick wall; if they don't know what's going on, they'll simply say that my illness has been **brought on** by stress. That causes me stress!
- A: She has been rather touchy recently about her relationship with her husband.
- B: What **brought that on**?

To show someone the ropes (To show someone how to do something/ how something works/where everything is)

Examples:
- Don't be cocky when she's **showing you the ropes**; it won't go down too well.
- I'll leave you in Peter's more than capable hands, taking you round the office; he's very adept at **showing people the ropes**.

Peckish (A little hungry)

Examples:
- He will only lift a finger with the cooking if he's feeling **peckish**.
- A: I'm a bit **peckish**; have you got anything to be getting on with? I haven't eaten all day.
- B: Oh stop whingeing!

Lesson Two

Grim (Severe, very depressing)

Examples:
- The plight of the hostages is, I'm afraid, looking rather **grim**.
- I think the **grim** winter weather must have brought on her flu.
I've lost track of how many of my patients are in the same situation.

Harass, harassment (To pick on--*see Practical Everyday English, page 103,* to bother someone continually, [harassment] persistent aggressive pressure/intimidation-- *often sexually or racially motivated. Note also that there is much dispute as to how this word should be pronounced. Traditionalists insist that the emphasis should be on the first 'a' ["harass, harassment"], but most people stress the second syllable [harass/harassment]. The author, however, is a traditionalist)*

Examples:
- As a child I felt I was constantly **harassed** by my mother for having inherited many of my father's traits.
- I alienated some of my classmates when I had a go at them about their racial **harassment** of my best friend.

To bond, a bond (To build up a close relationship with someone--often a parent or child, a close link)

Examples:
- Most new parents feel out of their depth when the baby comes along; they all need time to **bond**.
- You can see there is quite clearly a strong **bond** between father and son in this case. It all boils down to having watched their football team's grim decline in the league together.

To hold out a lot of/much hope (for someone) (To be optimistic--*generally used in the negative)*

Examples:
- Apparently, once in a blue moon, someone from his school gets into Oxford, but I **don't hold out a lot of hope (for him).**
- A: How is she, of all people, going to show the others the ropes? She's thick!
  B: I couldn't agree more; I **wouldn't hold out much hope for** any of them.

Sloppy (Careless, too casual)

Examples:
- I feel we've become too complacent lately and need to tighten up on **sloppy** work if we want to reap the rewards that are clearly on offer
- Football manager:
It's true we were overwhelmed in midfield, but our **sloppy** defence didn't help matters.

In hindsight (Looking back after the event)

Examples:
- **In hindsight**, we should have phased out the asylum laws a long time ago.
- I didn't hold out a lot of hope, but, **in hindsight**, I could have given her a lot more encouragement.
- It's very easy to say in **hindsight** we shouldn't have taken him on, but nobody would have predicted that he'd be so out of his depth in this type of business.

To put something behind you (To forget about a bad experience)

Examples:
- I think we should **put** the turmoil of the last year **behind us**; it's time to move on.
- A: If I had known he was such a womaniser, I would never have married him.

  B: It's probably best that you **put** that period of your life **behind you**.

To grow on someone (To become gradually more pleasing/likeable to someone)

Examples:
- At first you may find his mother's cooking rather bland, but don't despair: it's likely to **grow on you**.
- I used to think he was a bit pompous, but he has definitely **grown on** me over the years.

*"At first you may find his mother's cooking rather bland, but don't despair: it's likely to **grow on you**."*

(see page 109)

To sponge off someone (To keep asking/expecting someone to lend you money/pay for you, to rely on someone's/the state's generosity without appreciation/trying to find work)

Examples:
- *I really cut him down to size when I asked him if he felt it was right that, at thirty years old, he should still be **sponging off** his dad. He told me to shut up, as I was "doing his head in".*
- *I don't want to dwell on negative issues, but there are far too many people in this country **sponging off** the state…and some of them are raking it in.*

Viable (Practical, able to work in practice)

Examples:
- *I didn't think he had it in him to come up with so many **viable** ideas.*
- *My wife didn't relish the idea of opening another shop, and after reflecting on the hassles we went through with the first one, I agreed it wasn't really **viable**.*

L e s s o n   T h r e e

To flaunt (To show something off, especially wealth or physical attractiveness--*note the expression "If you've got it, flaunt it!"*)

> Examples:
> - I was totally overwhelmed when I first went to his massive house. It's quite apparent that his philosophy towards life is: If you've got it, ***flaunt*** it!
> - She doesn't find mingling with her male guests to be a problem; she just ***flaunts*** her legs at them…and their concentration tends to go astray.

*"I was totally overwhelmed when I first went to his massive house. It's quite apparent that his philosophy towards life is: If you've got it, **flaunt** it!"*

To leave a lot to be desired (To be not good enough, to be unsatisfactory)

> Examples:
> - The trumpet piece in this symphony has grown on me, but the percussion ***leaves a lot to be desired***.
> - I wouldn't hold out too much hope for him in his exams; his maths especially ***leaves a lot to be desired***.

On paper (In theory, according to records--*often used with "seems" or "looks"*)

Examples:
- **On paper**, the project <u>looks</u> viable, but in practice we're bound to have some teething problems.
- He <u>seemed</u> to be a good buy **on paper**, but after the first two matches, everyone could see that he was way out of his depth.

To know/find out what makes someone tick (To understand how someone's mind works, why they do certain things)

Examples:
- Even though there is quite definitely a bond between us and I'm looking forward to sharing a flat with her, I still don't **know what makes her tick**.
- He declined to go into much detail and just touched on the subject. I don't want to keep harassing him for more information, but I would dearly love to **find out what makes him tick**.

Broody

i. (Wanting to have a baby)
Examples:
- Seeing them flaunt their baby in front of everyone has made me feel **broody**.
- In hindsight, if my wife hadn't been so **broody**, we would never have had our second child, Tommy. Now we are both feeling very jaded, as he is so boisterous.

ii. (Unhappy because of too much thinking and deliberation--*note "**to brood over**"something means to become unhappy as a result of thinking about something too deeply—see "To dwell on" page 56*)
Examples:
- I don't know why he's being so **broody** about it; he should have put the whole episode behind him by now.
- There's no point in **brooding over** it. What on earth has brought this on?

To be well up on/with something (To be well informed--*note also the expression "to well up" which means to be about to cry or become more intense emotionally*)

Examples:
- I'm not really **well up** on how the company computer system works. So, I'm going to ask Sharon to show you the ropes. Sharon will be most enlightening...won't you, Sharon?
- Sorry, Peter, if this comes over as being tactless, but everyone at the meeting was **well up with** what was going on... apart from you.
- When she told me about how prudish her dad was, it reminded me of my dear grandfather. I suddenly started to **well up**.

Skint/Strapped for cash (Short of money, broke--*note "skint" is* **slang**)

Examples:
- I wouldn't bother trying to sponge off him; he's as **skint** as you are!
- On paper he's quite well-off, but, if truth be known, he's a bit **strapped for cash** and has trouble keeping his creditors at bay. He'll have to bluff his way through some difficult meetings next month.
- If I wasn't so **strapped for cash**, I would happily splash out with you at some posh restaurant in the City.

Plausible (Believable, possible)

Examples:
- The story about the sexual harassment he had supposedly suffered at work from some of his female colleagues was not very **plausible**; we still haven't got to the bottom of this.
- It is quite **plausible** that he didn't want to flaunt his house in front of the media because, in reality, he was rather strapped for cash.

To be chuffed (To be pleased, delighted) **Colloquial**

Examples:
- We were so **chuffed** when we heard that Susan was pregnant; we knew how broody she was after the birth of her niece.
- **"Chuffed"** is an understatement as to how I felt; more like "overwhelmed" with excitement. Success like this only happens to me once in a blue moon.

To be gutted   (To be very disappointed, devastated--*often used by sportsmen or their supporters to indicate how miserable they are feeling after losing*) **Colloquial**

Examples:
- Interviewer:
  *You must feel **gutted** after losing in the final for the second year in a row?*
  Tennis player:
  Well actually, it hasn't sunk in yet, but I'm not exactly chuffed about it, no.
- *I don't want to whinge about the referee, but how could he have deprived us of that goal? **Gutted**!*

TELEVISION DEBATE BETWEEN POLITICIANS

CHAIRMAN: *Good evening.*
Tonight in our London studio we have Janet Jones from the Government and Peter Smith from the Opposition. Could we have the first question from the audience please?

MEMBER OF AUDIENCE: *Concerning the plight of the asylum seekers currently requesting refuge in the UK, does the panel think that putting them in detention centres is a viable option, or should they be allowed to mingle with the local community?*

CHAIRMAN: *Peter Smith?*

PETER SMITH: *Well, I think the Government's recent policy on asylum leaves a lot to be desired. There are too many people sponging off the State as it is. I know the detention centre idea seems a bit grim and there are bound to be teething problems, but at present we are being overwhelmed by asylum seekers. Accepting more of them without restriction is quite unthinkable.*

CHAIRMAN: *I don't suppose you go along with that, Janet Jones?*

JANET JONES: *I most certainly do not; with right-wing ideology like that, I don't hold out much hope for Peter's party winning the next election. They have not come up with a plausible alternative to our liberal approach. However, in hindsight, I must admit we could have dealt with the problem differently. There was too much bureaucracy and too little action. But let's put that behind us now. We must stop the appalling harassment of these poor people by racist thugs and try to create a bond between the different communities which make up our country.*

PETER SMITH: *What ludicrous rubbish you are talking! Mind you, the British public are under no illusions about how things can only get much worse with Janet's party in power. Not long to go before the next general election when, ladies and gentlemen, you can put an end to your suffering.*

MARION: *Do you know, Jerry doesn't lift a finger to help in the house and yet, whenever we go to Anna's place for dinner, all she needs to do is flaunt her big brown eyes at him, and he becomes her slave…offering to wash the dishes…anything!*

PATRICIA: *Well, that's men for you! They all have the same traits. I know exactly what makes Steve tick; he maintains that his current broodiness has been brought on by Chelsea losing the Cup Final last week. He says he was gutted, but I know that the fact that he's completely skint after our holiday has meant that he can't afford to go out drinking with his mates. That's what's really getting to him.*

MARION: *But we couldn't do without them. I'd be so chuffed if Jerry decided to do the ironing one day. Perhaps the idea of housework will grow on him.*

PATRICIA: *Yes Marion. And pigs will fly!*

CHOOSE THE CORRECT WORD FROM THOSE IN RED
Answers on page 134

1. His wife was very cross with him because he never ª(created/lifted a finger/stepped in/ reimbursed) at home. ᵇ(In hindsight/Totally/On paper/At least), he could now see how all the problems started.

2. She has the ª(personalities/hindsight/traits/plight) of her mother; she also used to ᵇ(flaunt/ show off/sponge off/bond) herself at the opposite sex.

3. It's not really a ª(broody/peckish/grim/viable) option. We have to work out ᵇ(what makes them tick/how to sponge off them/to put it behind us/to be more plausible) before we can go on with negotiations.

4. He's quite ª(aware/grown/well up/skint) on European law, but I feel totally ᵇ(on the ropes/ mingled/chuffed/out of my depth).

5. A: Excuse me, but I must ª(overwhelm/mingle/have a go/lift a finger) with my other guests, otherwise they will think that my entertaining ᵇ(is wonderful/leaves a lot to be desired/is grim/has teething problems).
   B: You do that. But can I ask if there's any food around? I'm feeling a bit ᶜ(grim/skint/ chuffed/peckish).

6. ª(Gobsmacked/Mingling/On paper/In hindsight), it seemed to be a ᵇ(plausible/chuffed/ gutted/sloppy) idea, but the whole thing turned out to be a complete disaster.

7. A: The baby was crying all day yesterday.
   B: What ª(brought/turned/shrugged/stood) that on?
   A: Well, she's ᵇ(gutted/chuffed/teething/breathing) at the moment.
   B: Oh, all this talk about babies is making me feel ᶜ(skint/broody/plausible/peckish).

8. I must say that I felt a bit ª(gutted/broody/satisfied/overwhelmed) by all the information I had to take in on my first day at work. Luckily, Jean was there to ᵇ(show me the ropes/lift a finger/leave a lot to be desired/put it behind me).

9. Even though he's the sort of person who will think nothing of ª(bonding/sponging overwhelming/mingling) off his friends, I must admit he is beginning to ᵇ(annoy/sponge/ bond/grow) on me.

10. I know you feel ª(chuffed/gutted/broody/out of your depth) by these tragic events, but in the not too distant future you will be able to ᵇ(know what makes him tick/show him the ropes/put everything behind you/hold out a lot of hope).

11. *We weren't* ^a*(holding out too much hope/brooding/mingling/sponging) for her in these exams, and so we were really* ^b*(gutted/chuffed/grim/broody) when she told us that she had got into Cambridge.*

12. *After the relentless* ^a*(pleasure/traits/plight/harassment) she suffered as a child, it is heart-warming to see her* ^b*(uneasy/mingling/bonding/teething) with her mother again.*

13. *The* ^a*(uproar/harassment/plight/traits) of some African children is still looking* ^b*(grim/plausible/viable/skint). If I wasn't so* ^c*(harassed/strapped for cash/overwhelmed/gutted) at the moment, I would send them some money.*

Lesson One

Embroiled (Deeply involved in an argument, someone's problems or a difficult situation)

> Examples:
> * I don't want to get **embroiled** in another row, but his methods do leave a lot to be desired.
> * I wish we hadn't got so **embroiled** in his troubled personal life. Let's hope we can put it all behind us now.

To psych oneself up for/to do something (To prepare oneself mentally for a challenging situation)

> Examples:
> * Don't get me wrong; there's no rift between us, but these days I have to **psych myself up to** spend more than half an hour with my mother.
> * Anne doesn't think you should brood too much over tomorrow's meeting with your boss; I don't fully agree with her. I accept that you mustn't let it get to you, but you do need to **psych yourself up for** it.

Untoward (Something wrong, unexpected)

> Examples:
> * I thought there was something **untoward** when I saw the expression on her face but I didn't want to get embroiled in her relationship problems.
> * As my doctor is so well up on this area of medicine, I felt relieved when he told me that nothing **untoward** was going on.

To resent (To feel bitter about someone/a situation, to object to a comment, accusation or having to do something--*note the use of the gerund in the fourth example below--also note the noun "**resentment**"*)

> Examples:
> * My brother has always **resented** me for having had a better education than him. He's never quite been able to get it out of his system.

- A: *I reckon you don't want to buy your wife a birthday present because you're skint.*
- B: *I **resent** that remark!*
- *He **resented** the fact that I had accused him of taking his parents for granted over the last few years. In hindsight, I should have kept my mouth shut; I could see him welling up.*
- *Mum and I really **resent** having to grovel to the Headmaster to give you one last chance. Your behaviour is doing our heads in.*
- *Sarah's brother Fred flaunts his wealth at her whenever they are together. This behaviour is uncalled for as he knows that she is strapped for cash. No wonder she feels such **resentment** towards him.*

To have a bee in one's bonnet about something (To be preoccupied/obsessed with/troubled by something which often leads to complaining about it)

Examples:
- *She's got **a bee in her bonnet** about single mothers sponging off the state, but I think her own life leaves a lot to be desired.*
- *It's quite plausible that she couldn't put the whole thing behind her because she's still got **a bee in her bonnet** about her husband's string of affairs.*

To be doomed (To have no means of escape from a very bad situation, to have no future/chance of success)

Examples:
- *Most people I know don't hold out much hope for this country. We're **doomed**! I'm off to The Bahamas.*
- A: *I told you the project was **doomed** from the start.*
- B: *Yes, I must admit things are looking grim.*
- *Stock market investor: The Euro firstly had teething problems and now it's **doomed**…but I'm still buying it on the off-chance it might recover. I get a real buzz out of speculating.*

To put in a good word for someone (To recommend someone to another person/a group of people--*often used with regard to employment matters*)

Examples:
- *I was really chuffed to hear that John had **put in a good word for** me with my department manager. Until then I had been thinking about giving in my notice.*

- *She's the only one who knows what makes the boss tick. If she **puts in a good word for** you, he's bound to take you on.*

To browse (To look around a shop at one's leisure, not necessarily intending to buy anything)

Examples:
- *Our customers like to feel free to **browse** without any pressure from sales staff flaunting our products at them.*
- *There's nothing I like more on a Sunday afternoon than **browsing** around English village antique shops. I get a real kick out of bargain hunting.*

To stave off (To delay something unpleasant happening, to keep something unwanted at a distance)

Examples:
- *The doctors don't hold out much hope for her being able to **stave off** a return of the infection.*
- *Advertisement:*
  *If you're feeling peckish, why not try "Oaty Crisps"? They **stave off** hunger for up to three hours…and are kind to your waistline too.*

Apathy, apathetic (Lack of interest/motivation, uninterested/unconcerned)

Examples:
- *He resents his students not turning up to his lessons, and puts it all down to pure **apathy**. It's got nothing to do with him overwhelming them with work.*
- *Sorry to sound **apathetic**, but I couldn't care less whether he puts in a good word for me or not…and I'm certainly not going to grovel.*

*"Don't get me wrong; there's no rift between us, but these days I have to **psych myself up to** spend more than half an hour with my mother."*

(see page 119)

Lesson Two

To be flawed, a flaw (To be imperfect/To have faults, a defect/imperfection)

> Examples:
> - Their plans for the company are **flawed** in that they do not properly deal with the problem of staving off bankruptcy.
> - On paper, her ideas are quite plausible, but they have one major **flaw**: they don't take account of the general public's apathy toward local politics.

To embellish

i. (To add details to a story to make it sound more interesting/humorous)
> Examples:
> - A: He does tend to **embellish** his stories somewhat. I'd take everything he says with a large pinch of salt if I were you.
> - B: Why? You've definitely got it in for him, for some reason.
> - In the advert we're going to have to **embellish** the job details and what it entails; we don't want candidates to know we're dumbing down.

ii. (To decorate--*especially food rather than buildings*)
> Example:
> - I've got a bit of a bee in my bonnet about chefs who over-**embellish** their cakes with fruit.

To hamper (To restrict or interfere with the progress of something)

> Examples:
> - The police were severely **hampered** in their investigations by a crowd of people who were embroiled in a heated dispute.
> - We all psyched ourselves up for a long journey which would no doubt be **hampered** by the weather. My husband said we should have pre-empted this and left the day before, as he had suggested. He was clearly welling up with resentment towards me.

To linger, lingering (To take a long time leaving a place/To stay in the area and not go away quickly, long-lasting, remaining)

Examples:
- We **lingered** over lunch, embellishing old memories of our childhood together. I don't think we were deprived of much.
- The general impression I got is that customers are welcome to browse…but not **linger** for too long.
- Doctor to patient: It's quite feasible that you have had a **lingering** virus that has made you feel a bit under the weather…but there's nothing untoward to worry about.
- If you have any **lingering** doubts and are still feeling a bit sceptical, let me know and I'll take you through the proceedings once again.

Overall (Taking things altogether/by and large--*usually followed by something positive*)

Examples:
- **Overall**, we shouldn't really complain; they did try to make amends for what they had done.
- There were a few flaws with the design, but **overall** we were quite chuffed with the results.

Outburst (Sudden showing of emotions/feelings)

Examples:
- The media are quite clearly trying to cash in on the Princess's death, but the public are in no mood to curb this **outburst** of grief.
- There was an **outburst** of applause when the actress flaunted her baby in front of her adoring fans.

To allege, alleged, allegedly (To accuse, claim, declare without proof, [alleged] accused, [allegedly] supposedly--*often used by people in the media to protect themselves from being sued, i.e. when they don't have 100% proof of their **allegation***)

Examples:
- It is **alleged** that the defendant pestered Miss Jones for many years, despite his claim that he had turned over a new leaf.
- She **alleges** that her husband perpetually beat her. Be under no illusions: their marriage was flourishing until she took to dabbling in drugs.
- The **alleged** thief apparently thrived on causing uproar in the village.

- A: *His mother built him up to be something he wasn't, and too often gave him the benefit of the doubt. He's a cocky liar.*
- B: ***Allegedly!***

To be shattered

i. (To be very tired)
Examples:
- *I resent having to get up early at the weekends; I'm **shattered** by Friday.*
- *Let's not linger over dinner tonight; I'm **shattered** and could do with an early night.*

ii. (To be shocked/devastated/distressed by news)
Examples:
- *After being broody for so long, she was **shattered** by the news that she can't have children. She and her husband had been clutching at straws over the last few years.*
- *The company's employees were all **shattered** when they discovered that many of the directors had been raking it in while they had been struggling to make ends meet.*

iii. (To be smashed to pieces)
Examples:
- *The firemen were hampered in their work because all the windows in the house had been **shattered**.*
- *She'd been stringing him along all these years and now his dreams are **shattered**.*

To deem (To consider/think, to declare--*often something negative or difficult to accept*)

Examples:
- *After weighing up all the options, the headteacher **deemed** it necessary to get rid of all the disruptive pupils in the school.*
- *The Government's plans to revitalise the National Health Service were **deemed** to be implausible by the Opposition.*

To blur, blurred (To affect one's vision, to make something unclear, [blurred] distorted/unclear)

Examples:
- Alcohol lingers in the blood stream for 24 hours and can **blur** your vision…and then you might write your car off if you drive.
- The Ministry of Defence have bowed to pressure put on them by the Prime Minister to come up with a statement about Iraq. Many commentators believe that the truth has been **blurred**.
- Everything suddenly went **blurred** and the next thing I knew was that I had passed out. To say I was scared is something of an understatement.

"We **lingered** over lunch, embellishing old memories of our childhood together. I don't think we were deprived of much"

(see page 123)

Lesson Three

To console, consolation (To offer one's sympathy, to make someone feel better emotionally in times of sadness, a small positive thing that happens in a negative situation)

Examples:
- I tried to **console** her, but she was clearly shattered by the sad news.
- We were **consoled** by the fact that somehow we had managed to stave off defeat for so long…and we did get a **consolation** goal.
- For me it was no **consolation** for the loss of my job that an increased redundancy pay was a viable option.

Gut reaction (Immediate reaction/response based on instinct rather than careful consideration)

Examples:
- My **gut reaction** was to resent his accusations, and I had a real go at him. Later, when I realised he had in fact put in a good word for me with my manager, I regretted not having given the matter more thought.
- His outburst of anger was just a **gut reaction**, but when he had calmed down, he decided that it was better not to make a big song and dance about it. It was the first time his teenage son had come home paralytic.

Blip (An unexpected and temporary change from the normal situation)

Examples:
- It looks like we're strapped for cash this month. I hope it's just a **blip** and that business picks up in the next quarter.
- Book sales have gone through the roof this August. It could just be a summer **blip**, so let's not get too carried away before embarking on a second edition.

Banter (Chat, informal witty conversation amongst friends)

Examples:
- I used to enjoy the **banter** with the guys after the game, but now, in my old age, I'm becoming rather apathetic about socialising.
- The **banter** in the office is excellent, although Graham's poor grammar does grate on me.

To ad-lib, ad-libbed (To make something up on the spot, to speak in public without preparation, improvised)

Examples:
- My gut reaction was that I should **ad-lib** the speech rather than linger too long over making notes.
- It was quite clear that most of the banter on the TV show was **ad-libbed**. I'm always amazed at how much funny material they can come up with on the spot.

Hopeful (Optimistic--note that "I'm **hopeful** of passing my exams" is not the same as "I hope I pass my exams". "To be hopeful" expresses a feeling of optimism, whereas "to hope" is simply to desire)

Examples:
- I'm not very **hopeful** of being able to console her; her view of the future is somewhat blurred by recent events.
- Overall, he's quite **hopeful** of being able to deal with the allegations laid before him.

To tar people with the same brush (To claim a group of people have the same faults--used when a majority of good characters are associated with one or a few bad characters, just because they are of the same race, age, gender, class etc)

Examples:
- These two boys, who clearly have some very unpleasant traits in their personalities, have been mingling with some very dodgy characters indeed. But it would be quite wrong to **tar** the whole class **with the same brush**.
- **Tarring** all immigrants to this country with **the same brush** is ludicrous, and will only serve to alienate them further from the society in which they now live.

To be prone to (To have a tendency towards a certain type of negative behaviour, to be likely to suffer from)

Examples:
- He is rather **prone to** outbursts of bad temper. This is a flaw in his character which he inherited from his mother.
- In her youth she was **prone to** getting ear infections. This was deemed by her pathetic doctor to be the cause of her current fatigue problems. And doctors wonder why we constantly whinge about them!

To endear oneself to someone, endearing (To make oneself popular, [endearing] likeable)

Examples:
- The Prime Minister didn't **endear himself** to the medical profession when he complained that far too many doctors displayed an apathetic attitude towards their patients…and were raking it in.
- She has many **endearing** qualities, one of which is the ability not to dwell for too long on negative aspects of her life, unlike her pessimistic mother. They are like chalk and cheese.

Not to have a leg to stand on (To have no defence at all to an alleged crime or accusation)

Examples:
- He is quite hopeful of being found not guilty, but most of us think he **hasn't a leg to stand on** and should change his plea.
- My gut reaction is that you should back down. It's good that you've now got it out of your system, but if it ends up in court, you won't **have a leg to stand on**.

*"He is quite hopeful of being found not guilty, but most of us think he **hasn't a leg to stand on** and should change his plea."*

C h a p t e r   N i n e   **i n   U s e**

TWO STUDENTS DISCUSSING EXAMS

JOHN: *I have to say, I really resent having to study for chemistry, even though I'm quite hopeful of getting through the exam.*

MARIA: *I must say these days I have a rather apathetic attitude towards the sciences. In last year's physics exam I tried to embellish my answers with irrelevant philosophical views on the laws of nature. My arguments must have been flawed because I failed miserably. Any ambitions my dad has of me becoming a scientist like him are doomed, I'm afraid.*

JOHN: *Well, this year I'll try to put in a good word for you with Miss Austin, the physics teacher, although she has probably tarred all of us with the same brush.*

MARIA: *I don't know if it'll make any difference. I'm finding it harder and harder each year to psych myself up for exams. I'm not sure what career path I want to take either. Everything is looking a bit blurred at the moment.*

JOHN: *But not bleak! Whatever brought this sudden outburst on? You seem to have got a bee in your bonnet about exams, but I think you're being too hard on yourself. Your recent poor performance in exams is probably just a blip, don't you think? Overall, you've got everything going for you. Don't let a lack of confidence shatter all your dreams.*

MARIA: *Thanks John. You're a real mate.*

Last week I was *browsing* through one of the Sunday newspapers when I noticed an article about a new alternative treatment for *staving off* viruses.

Apparently, rubbing banana peel into one's nose twice a day is supposed to fight off any *lingering* virus which may be *hampering* a full recovery after a period of fatigue and malaise.

In the last few years I have been *prone to* coming down with infections, so my *gut reaction* was: "Why not give it a go?" Initially nothing happened. Then I started to sneeze violently and feel nauseous.

I became very upset as yet another alternative therapy proved to be a complete waste of time and money. My wife tried to *console* me, but I believe there is something *untoward* about these non-doctors trying to *endear* themselves to a gullible and vulnerable public, many of whom are desperate to find a cure for their ills.

I don't want to get *embroiled* in legal disputes, but if I were to sue any of these cheats over what they *allege* to be medicine, they wouldn't *have a leg to stand on*.

Chapter Nine: **Exercise**

CHOOSE THE CORRECT WORD FROM THOSE IN RED
Answers on page 134

1. Breaking even was ᵃ(resented/deemed/alleged/endeared) to be impossible this year, but my ᵇ(gut reaction/embellishment/resentfulness/plight) was that we were always going to make it.

2. I really enjoy all the ᵃ(outbursts/apathy/banter/fun) with the lads at work. ᵇ(Resenting/Consoling/Getting a bee in our bonnets/Ad-libbing) is something that comes as second nature to us guys.

3. Even though I had ᵃ(psyched myself up/consoled myself/deemed it necessary/endeared myself) for a massive row with my parents, in the end I decided I didn't want to get ᵇ(shattered/embroiled/consoled/resented) in their marital problems.

4. Unfortunately, the company has been ᵃ(shattered/doomed/staved off/blurred) since the beginning of last year. The fact that their products were still selling was no ᵇ(banter/outburst/consolation/gut reaction) to the staff who all had to be laid off.

5. The play ᵃ(ad-libbed/continued/stood/lingered) on seemingly without an end, and the audience became more and more ᵇ(apathetic/endearing/blurred/hopeful) towards what was happening onstage.

6. ᵃ(In total/Nevertheless/Alleged/Overall), the medical profession agree with the proposed changes to patient care, but they do ᵇ(are hopeful of/stave off/resent/psych themselves up to) interference from politicians. Just because they may come across the occasional bad doctor, it doesn't entitle them to ᶜ(tar everyone with the same brush/have a bee in their bonnet/browse/be flawed).

7. When it was ᵃ(accused/alleged/resented/embellished) that he had done something ᵇ(untoward/endearing/hopeful/apathetic), he was absolutely ᶜ(hampered/blurred/shattered/embroiled).

8. John not being drunk last week was just a ᵃ(consolation/banter/blip/outburst). He's usually paralytic by 2pm everyday, and from then on everything else becomes a ᵇ(hopeful/blurred/deemed/embroiled) memory.

9. I must admit I was surprised by her sudden ᵃ(gut reaction/consolation/outburst/embellishment) today, even though I knew she had a ᵇ(trait/banter/bee in her bonnet/consolation) about the way things are being run.

10. I'm quite ᵃ(reluctant/apathetic/hopeful/hampered) that we will be able to ᵇ(psych ourselves up for/shatter/resent/stave off) bankruptcy for at least another year.

11. A: *If you could* ^a*(console/resent/ad-lib/put in a good word) for my daughter, I'd be most grateful.*
B: *With pleasure, but I don't think it will be necessary with the* ^b*(endearing/resentful/ browsing/untoward) qualities she has already shown she has.*

12. *In this business we often find customers are* ^a*(hopeful/prone/deemed/apathetic) to* ^b*(endearing/embellishing/browsing/blurring) with absolutely no intention of buying anything.*

13. *As the defendant began to* ^a*(embellish/resent/blur/linger) his story to the court, it became clear to those of us in the jury that he hadn't* ^b*(put in a good word/got a leg to stand on/ any consolation/any banter).*

14. *The architect said that the project was* ^a*(hampered/resented/staved off/shattered) by appalling weather conditions. However, I honestly believe his plans were* ^b*(ad-libbed/ flawed/untoward/endearing) from the very beginning.*

Answers to Exercises

Chapter One
1(a) scapegoat; (b) dogsbody; 2(a) go by; (b) hardship; 3(a) on record; (b) up and coming; (c) get a lot of stick; 4(a) had it in you; (b) rubbed him up the wrong way; 5(a) breaking even; (b) came through; 6(a) pencil you in; (b) backlog; (c) bogged down; 7(a) Off the record; (b) loopholes; (c) baffled; 8(a) outgoing; (b) understatement;   (c) cocky; 9(a) in his element; (b) clichés; (c) touchy; 10(a) going around; (b) layout; 11(a) up in the air; (b) keep you posted; 12(a) at stake; (b) brush up.

Chapter Two
1(a) Deep down; (b) came to light; (c) complying with; 2(a) sulk; (b) wimp; 3(a) asking after; (b) have a lot on your plate; 4(a) gist; (b) nip it in the bud; (c) stumbling blocks; 5(a) By no stretch of the imagination; (b) miss out on; 6(a) wrote off; (b) final straw; (c) weighing everything up; 7(a) Once in a blue moon; (b) boils down; 8(a) down-to-earth; (b) keep a low profile; 9(a) drew out; (b) shrugged it off; 10(a) outnumbered; (b) miss the boat; (c) warranted; 11(a) drawing in; (b) lay on; 12(a) foregone conclusion; (b) over the top; (c) blow over; 13(a) jumping on the bandwagon; (b) by any stretch of the imagination.

Chapter Three
1(a) butt in; (b) waffling on; 2(a) to make ends meet; (b) by and large; (c) stood him in good stead; 3(a) uneasy; (b) disruptive; (c) bring out the best; 4(a) bland; (b) tactful; 5(a) corner the market; (b) bear in mind; (c) outlook; 6(a) lull us into a false sense of security; (b) complacency; 7(a) play down; (b) enlightening; 8(a) sticks out like a sore thumb; (b) clutching at straws; 9(a) budge; (b) prudish; 10(a) Take my word for it;   (b) streetwise; (c) laughing stock; 11(a) turn-off; (b) put it past her; 12(a) touched on; (b) grow out of; 13(a) comes in phases; (b) stick it out.

Chapter Four
1(a) take the mickey out of; (b) pompous; 2(a) like chalk and cheese; (b) gets flustered; 3(a) inadvertently; (b) unrest; (c) comeuppance; 4(a) Amidst; (b) passed out; (c) distraught; 5(a) lost track; (b) playing me up; (c) handful; 6(a) dwell; (b) give him the benefit of the doubt; 7(a) go astray; (b) get my head round; 8(a) get to the bottom of; (b) skim the surface; (c) reap the rewards; 9(a) gobsmacked; (b) raking it in; 10(a) passé; (b) stilted; 11(a) get a real kick out of; (b) squeamish; 12(a) get it out of my system; (b) past it; (c) stranded.

Chapter Five
1(a) yobs; (b) get a buzz out of; (c) frenzied; 2(a) under no illusions; (b) bluffing your way through; 3(a) pledge; (b) dwindling; (c) down to; 4(a) shortlist; (b) fiasco; 5(a) cram; (b) doing my head in; 6(a) adept; (b) building; (c) pathetic; 7(a) perpetual; (b) pre-empt; 8(a) grovelling; (b) wallow: 9(a) backed down; (b) upsurge; 10(a) aftermath; (b) makeshift; (c) huddle together; 11(a) boisterous; (b) on cue: (c) off his rocker; 12(a) jaded; (b) phased in; (c) makes a mockery of.

Chapter Six
1(a) bitter pill to swallow; (b) take us through; 2(a) hype; (b) grounding; (c) dumbed-down; 3(a) undermine; (b) alienate him; (c) endowed with; 4(a) string me; (b) blatant;   (c) not on; 5(a) unnerves; (b) disgruntled; 6 (a) slapdash; (b) strays; 7(a) emerged; (b) go for a song; (c) keep at bay; 8(a) branded; (b) comeback; (c) slim; 9(a) shift;   (b) unveil; 10(a) pushover; (b) pester; (c) grate; 11(a) skirmishes; (b) amend; 12(a) uproar; (b) died down.

Chapter Seven
1(a) curbed; (b) paralytic; (c) rub it in; 2(a) embarked on; (b) sceptical; 3(a) dark horse; (b) deprive you; (c) spoken for; 4(a) bolshy; (b) you've got another think coming; (c) thrives on; 5(a) make a song and dance about it; (b) sap; (c) flourishing; 6(a) envisage; (b) whingeing; 7(a) beggars belief; (b) scraping the barrel; (c) give her a taste of her own medicine; 8(a) dabbles; (b) rift; (c) banging his head against a brick wall; 9(a) make a beeline; (b) sucker for punishment; 10(a) turned over a new leaf; (b) go over his head; 11(a) head off; (b) turmoil; 12(a) cashed in on; (b) bowed to pressure.

Chapter Eight
1(a) lifted a finger; (b) In hindsight; 2(a) traits; (b) flaunt; 3(a) viable; (b) what makes them tick; 4(a) well-up; (b) out of my depth; 5(a) mingle; (b) leaves a lot to be desired; (c) peckish; 6(a) On paper; (b) plausible; 7(a) brought; (b) teething; (c) broody; 8(a) overwhelmed; (b) show me the ropes; 9(a) sponging; (b) grow; 10(a) gutted; (b) put everything behind you; 11(a) holding out too much hope; (b) chuffed; 12(a) harassment; (b) bonding; 13(a) plight; (b) grim; (c)strapped for cash.

Chapter Nine
1(a) deemed; (b) gut reaction; 2(a) banter; (b) ad-libbing; 3(a) psyched myself up; (b) embroiled; 4(a) doomed; (b) consolation; 5(a) lingered; (b) apathetic; 6(a) Overall; (b) resent; (c) tar everyone with the same brush; 7(a) alleged; (b) untoward; (c) shattered; 8(a) blip; (b) blurred; 9(a) outburst; (b) bee in her bonnet; 10(a) hopeful; (b) stave off; 11(a) put in a good word; (b) endearing; 12(a) prone; (b) browsing; 13(a) embellish; (b) a leg to stand on; 14(a) hampered; (b) flawed.

Index

LETTER **W**

LETTER **Y**